AUTHORITATIVE GUIDE TO

Pinhooking for Profit

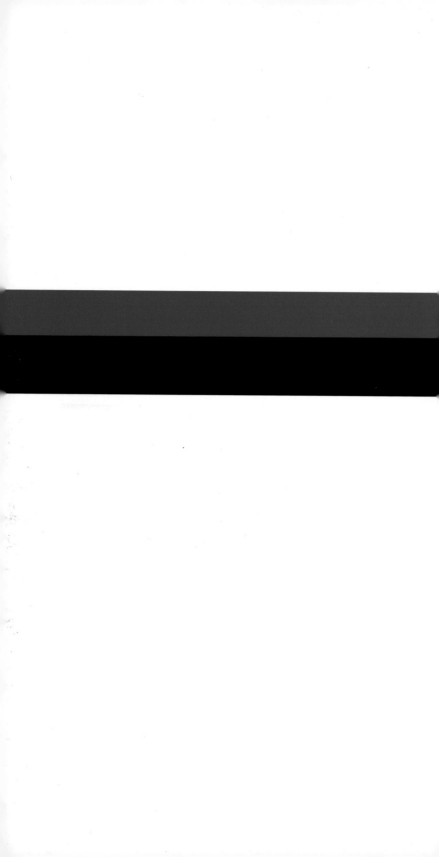

THE
Blood-Horse

AUTHORITATIVE GUIDE TO

Pinhooking for Profit

**BY THE STAFF AND CORRESPONDENTS
OF BLOOD-HORSE PUBLICATIONS**

Lexington, Kentucky

ECLIPSE
PRESS

Library of Congress Control Number: 2006928171

ISBN-13: 978-1-58150-145-2
ISBN-10: 1-58150-145-5

Printed in China
First Edition: 2006

Distributed to the trade by
National Book Network
4501 Forbes Blvd., Suite 200, Lanham, MD 20706
1.800.462.6420

A Division of
Blood-Horse Publications
Publishers Since 1916

ECLIPSE
PRESS

Contents

COVER PHOTOGRAPH BY ANNE M. EBERHARDT

Overview of Pinhooking

Many people who follow the Thoroughbred industry have read about the incredible pinhooking tour de force that took place in 2006 when Floridians Randy Hartley and Dean De Renzo sold a two-year-old colt at Fasig-Tipton for a heart-pounding $16 million after buying the horse eleven months earlier for $425,000 — a price that seemed high at the time. Though Hartley outwardly reassured De Renzo they hadn't paid too much for the Forestry—Magical Masquerade yearling, both men couldn't help but inwardly question the logic of spending nearly a half-million dollars on a horse still too young to set hoof on the track.

But when the Fasig-Tipton gavel came down at the Florida select sale of two-year-olds in training, Hartley and De Renzo looked like geniuses. The two horsemen, who have been partners for more than fifteen years, staggered away, weak-kneed, with a profit of more than $15 million.

A story such as this might inspire some to get into the pinhooking business, but the odds of repeating such a feat fall in line with the odds of winning the Triple Crown.

Ultimate home run: the $16 million Forestry—Magical Masquerade colt.

ELIOT J. SCHECHTER

LESLIE MARTIN

Two-year-olds ready to race represent the majority of pinhook prospects.

In fact, only about half of all pinhooked horses are even profitable. More than one-third of the time pinhookers end up buying back their horses at auction because they did not bring their reserve price.

The pinhooking market is fickle, not only from year to year but also from segment to segment. Whether it's buying weanlings to sell as yearlings, yearlings to sell as two-year-olds, or broodmare prospects to sell as broodmares, pinhooking is a game of high risk with the potential for high reward. Most people who get into it as a career, investment, or sideline should have the wherewithal to withstand ups and downs, not to mention having the prerequisite good eye for horses.

This guide explores all aspects of pinhooking from different angles to give readers an overall picture of the business and a blueprint for getting started. *The Blood-Horse Authoritative Guide to Pinhooking for Profit* also has sought the expertise

of successful people in the field who offer advice and warn of the pitfalls they have encountered in their many years in the business. Pinhooking isn't easy, but if done properly and cautiously, it is a business that can reap much satisfaction and financial reward.

The term pinhooking was coined in the early 1900s when a speculator with a roll of greenbacks would buy tobacco from cash-strapped farmers before they took their burley to market. In the jargon of Thoroughbred sales, the term now refers to buying a horse with the sole purpose of selling it for a profit later. A majority of pinhookers buy yearlings to sell as two-year-olds ready to race. The idea is to speculate on a young horse, in one of its most formative years, before a career at the track renders final judgment.

Compared to other segments of the Thoroughbred industry, pinhooking as a profession is relatively new. Many people who pinhooked before the 1980s did so as a means of supplementing their breeding businesses, not as a sole source of income. In the early 1990s, as the market for two-year-olds in training grew, more men and women turned pinhooking into full-time jobs.

"It started offering an opportunity to make a living," said Jimmy Gladwell of Ocala, Florida, who grew up raising Quarter Horses but got into pinhooking Thoroughbreds in 1979 when he saw more of an opportunity to make money. "The supply and demand was there."

Many pinhookers are based around Ocala, Florida, but often buy their yearlings at the Keeneland September yearling sale in Lexington, Kentucky, where the

bulk of Thoroughbred breeding takes place. These yearlings usually are broken, trained, and prepared in Florida for one of the state's many two-year-old sales. California and Kentucky also host major two-year-old sales.

How much pinhookers invest in their horses and how many they

Ocala, Florida, is home to many pinhookers.

9

buy vary. Some pinhookers team with partners to increase buying power and to obtain more horses and spread the risk. Buying horses at the top of the market or at the bottom of the market brings the most risk. With cheap horses, there's no guarantee a pinhooker will make enough money to cover the upkeep (estimated at about $9,000 a year), breaking and training, and preparation of a horse for auction unless the horse undergoes a radical transformation under the pinhooker's regime. At the top level, there's also no guarantee a large investment is going to pay off.

In fact, at the same Fasig-Tipton select two-year-olds sale at which Hartley and De Renzo earned enough to buy their own private island, several sellers lost money on higher-end horses. For example, a Grand Slam—Susie Ticket colt purchased for $310,000 as a yearling sold for $40,000.

"We have a lot of money in these horses, and there's a large amount of information available to the buyers on them," Florida pinhooker Terry Oliver of O & H Bloodstock told *The Blood-Horse* after the Fasig-Tipton sale. "We breeze them very fast down the racetrack, and some of them are going to pay on the vetting. All the buyers want the best horses they can get, and it's easy for them to fall off of one that has a little bit of this problem or a little bit of that problem. If a horse has a sub-par video or a sub-par work, he becomes a sub-par horse. What you had to pay for them as yearlings doesn't matter. There have been some years where we've scratched our heads and gone back home on a credit card."

Being that experts in the business for years still can't always master the market should indicate that pinhooking is not for the faint of heart. What might seem simple at first glance — buying and selling horses — involves a lot of attention to both the big picture and the small picture, not to mention a lot of luck. Young horses, like young children, love to play, and injury, sickness, or unforeseen circumstances might squelch the best-laid plans.

Newcomers to the business should take a hard look at what's involved and educate themselves not only on pedigree, conformation, and a horse's potential for improvement, but also on types of pinhooking, trends, upkeep costs, sales preparation, and marketing. *The Blood-Horse Authoritative Guide to Pinhooking for Profit* offers a good starting point and reference for anyone trying to get a leg up in the business.   — *Rena Baer*

Types of Pinhooking

This chapter discusses the different types of pinhooking and the advantages and disadvantages associated with each. In addition, the chapter advises the prospective buyer to prepare for a sale by enlisting the help of experts, learning how to read a catalog page, and becoming familiar with how an auction company conducts business.

Weanling to Yearling

How to: Pinhooking weanlings (horses weaned from their mothers between four and six months of age) is a relatively new development in the Thoroughbred industry, and no auctions are dedicated solely to selling these youngsters. Weanlings are usually purchased at mixed or breeding stock sales, conducted in late fall and early winter. (See appendix for list of auctions.)

Sixty percent of all weanlings sold in North America come from the Keeneland November breeding stock sale, a two-week marathon offering all levels of pedigree, conformation, and price. In 2005, buyers purchased 1,087 weanlings from this sale as compared to 324 at the second-largest weanling sale, Ocala Breeders' Sales Company fall mixed sale. The median price (50 percent above and 50 below) for a weanling in 2005 was $15,000, but the range is huge, starting at less than $1,000 and sometimes surpassing $1 million (which is why

ANNE M. EBERHARDT

A weanling in the sales ring.

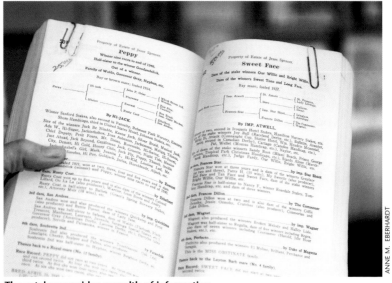

The catalog provides a wealth of information.

median prices can be a more accurate gauge of the market.).

To get started in pinhooking, you must put together a plan and decide how much money you want to spend and whether you would rather buy more less-expensive horses or fewer expensive horses. Or you might decide you want to dabble in pinhooking as an investor in a partnership. Everyone's budgets and goals are different, so this is a very individual choice though experts recommend you spread the risk by investing in more horses rather than a single costly one. If that one gets hurt, there is no way to recoup the loss.

The first few days of most major sales usually yield the cream of the crop ("select" horses) and therefore bring higher bids. As the sale progresses, median prices drop each day, and toward the end prices are often comparable to what can be found in smaller, more regional sales that serve the breeding and racing industry in specific areas.

With thousands of horses to choose from, both at auctions and in private transactions, it's integral for you to enlist the help of a reputable adviser — perhaps a bloodstock agent, trainer, farm manager, or consignor — to find the right sale and the right horse.

Every sale has its own catalog, with a page dedicated to each horse being auctioned (see page 16) on how to read a catalog page. The page will show all kinds of pertinent information, including hip number, pedigree, notable progeny of the sire and dam, and race records of the most prominent family members. An adviser should be able to help you comb through this information to come up with a list of prospects that look like they'll offer value for price. From this list, the two of you will be able to decide which horses you want to inspect before the sale.

This inspection is the opportunity to check out a horse's conformation (physical make-up), a component very important to pinhookers. You'll have a chance to see if anything about the horse's build could potentially impede its ability to run and, hence, its ability to sell as a yearling. It takes years of observing to make accurate judgments about very young horses, so make sure you have an adviser who knows Thoroughbreds. Some weanlings may outgrow certain conformational flaws as they gain more muscle while other conformational flaws may worsen with time. Yet others may be corrected with surgery. It takes an expert to know the difference among the three. (Also, it is imperative to have a veterinarian check out a prospect's X-rays to make sure the horse is sound. Some sales require this so that a horse cannot be returned for a problem disclosed in the X-rays.)

In addition, an adviser should be able to spot potential and help

> ### THINGS TO KNOW
>
> It is wise to enlist the expertise of reputable advisers to find the right horse for pinhooking opportunities.
>
> Yearling buyers focus on conformation, looks, and pedigree while purchasers of two-year-olds focus more on the timed works.
>
> A good pedigree is important for a broodmare prospect.

you get the best bang for your buck. Buying weanlings for resale is akin to choosing which third-graders will become standout high school athletes.

Buyers also can do further research on family lines and family race records through The Jockey Club Information Systems' Equineline (www.equineline.com), Bloodstock Research (www.brisnet.com), and *The Blood-Horse* magazine (www.bloodhorse.com) to gain as much insight into a

ANNE M. EBERHARDT

Weanlings need space to run and grow once they have been purchased.

prospect as possible. Does a candidate have any other siblings on the track? How have they performed? How many mares did the stallion breed, and will the market be oversaturated with his progeny, driving down their resale value? There are many considerations for you to weigh with an adviser before coming up with that short list of hip numbers to bid on.

Before heading to an auction, you will need to understand how it operates and the conditions of sale, which address credit and payment, responsibilities of the buyer and seller, warranties concerning soundness, and the resolution of disputes. These conditions are usually included in the sales catalog and should be read carefully. Also, keep in mind that once the auction hammer falls, the horse changes hands. You are now liable for the horse and should immediately arrange transportation and insurance, tasks you also can do beforehand.

Before buying weanlings, you must arrange a place to board them (fees usually range from $8 to $38 a day per horse) or have your own farm to keep them on. These young horses need space to run and let their bodies develop. They also need to be handled daily — hand walking, foot care, grooming — to prepare them for sales and the breaking and training that will take place the following year. For an additional charge, some farms manage weanlings and prepare them for resale as yearlings. Or, a consignor can be hired to help prepare the horse for resale. A consignor will offer suggestions on a horse's appearance and advice on which sales he or she thinks would reap the best return and where in the sale you should request your

horse be placed. Consignors also can suggest a reserve price that will keep the horse from being sold should the bids not be high enough. Their job is to help prepare your horse for resale so that it brings the highest price possible, thus earning the consignor larger commissions.

Without any timed workouts or trials to base their decisions upon, yearling buyers look at conformation, appearance, and pedigree. The best thing a weanling-to-yearling pinhooker can do is give these young horses every opportunity to flourish over this growth-filled year, present them in their best light at auction, and hope that an older sibling or half sibling proves itself on the track, upping the value of the family line.

Advantages: The main advantage of pinhooking weanlings to yearlings is that the risk is not as high as it is in other segments of the pinhooking market. A fairly well-conformed, well-chosen weanling usually will be a well-conformed, well-received yearling. Not yet in training, these young horses don't have the opportunity to turn off buyers with their running styles and are also less apt to injure themselves than horses in training. Weanlings also don't require the added expense of breaking and training that comes with buying a yearling to resell as a two-year-old.

Disadvantages: While pinhooking weanlings to yearlings is less risky, it doesn't usually reap huge windfalls. Weanlings bought for an average of $56,258 in 2004 were pinhooked as yearlings for an average of $76,780 in 2005, a rate of return of 39 percent. Compare this

Good conformation is a must in a pinhooking prospect.

with yearlings bought for an average of $76,392 in 2004 and pinhooked as two-year-olds for an average of $165,090 in 2005, an 82 percent rate of return.

Also, the yearling market is huge (10,088 sold in 2005) compared to the weanling market (1,824) and two-year-old market (3,137). Young horses historically have been sold as yearlings, plus some people may sell yearlings in an attempt to cull any surplus youngsters that may not look promising as racehorses before they shell out the money to break and train them and have their suspicions proven.

Yearling to Two-year-old

How to: The largest segment of the pinhooking business is buying yearlings to resell as two-year-olds. Most pinhooked yearlings are purchased at the Keeneland September yearling sale, another mammoth two-week auction that offers a wide variety of youngsters. Though the Keeneland yearling sale is by far the largest, a multitude of yearling sales take place throughout the country, primarily between August and October. Yearlings (or any other age Thoroughbred) also can be purchased privately at any time through classified ads or, on rare occasion, at auctions through private deals. Yearling prices can start at under $1,000 but can climb higher than $9 million on rare occasion.

Much of the research advice and protocol for buying a yearling to sell as a two-year-old is the same as choosing a weanling to pinhook as a yearling, except at this stage the horse will be tested as a runner

How to read a catalog page

A catalog page can seem confusing and intimidating at first glance. What do all those names and terms mean and how do you use them? But don't worry. Use these pointers to familiarize yourself with a horse's catalog page, and you will quickly learn to interpret the information to help you decide which horse you want. Here, an example of a yearling catalog page is shown.

1 The number identifying the horse, appearing on its hip.

2 The horse's pedigree, traced three generations. At each generation the sire appears on the top and the dam on the bottom.

3 A synopsis of the sire's racing record and notable progeny.

4 A synopsis of the first dam's racing record and progeny.

5 The maternal grandmother.

6 A synopsis of the racing record of the second dam's most prominent offspring. Each indentation represents one generation.

7 The maternal great-grandmother.

8 Many states have special racing opportunities restricted to horses bred in their state. This will indicate if the horse is eligible for such a program.

9 A listing of upcoming stakes races to which the horse has been nominated.

10 Bold capital letters for a horse's name indicate the horse is a stakes winner. If its name appears in bold lower-case letters, the horse is stakes-placed.

11 The horse's birth date.

12 The horse's name. If unnamed, the horse is described by sex and color.

13 The name of the consignor (the farm or individual selling the horse).

14 Indicates the stakes race is graded and which grade.

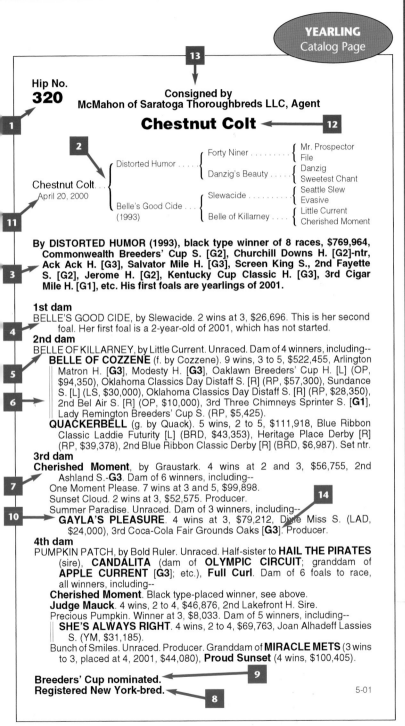

13

Hip No.
320

Consigned by
McMahon of Saratoga Thoroughbreds LLC, Agent

1

Chestnut Colt ← **12**

2

Chestnut Colt...
April 20, 2000

11

Distorted Humor . . . .
- Forty Niner . . . .
  - Mr. Prospector
  - File
- Danzig's Beauty . . . . .
  - Danzig
  - Sweetest Chant

Belle's Good Cide . . . .
(1993)
- Slewacide . . . .
  - Seattle Slew
  - Evasive
- Belle of Killarney . . . .
  - Little Current
  - Cherished Moment

By **DISTORTED HUMOR** (1993), black type winner of 8 races, $769,964, Commonwealth Breeders' Cup S. **[G2]**, Churchill Downs H. **[G2]**-ntr, Ack Ack H. **[G3]**, Salvator Mile H. **[G3]**, Screen King S., 2nd Fayette S. **[G2]**, Jerome H. **[G2]**, Kentucky Cup Classic H. **[G3]**, 3rd Cigar Mile H. **[G1]**, etc. His first foals are yearlings of 2001.

3

1st dam
BELLE'S GOOD CIDE, by Slewacide. 2 wins at 3, $26,696. This is her second foal. Her first foal is a 2-year-old of 2001, which has not started.

4

2nd dam
BELLE OF KILLARNEY, by Little Current. Unraced. Dam of 4 winners, including--
  BELLE OF COZZENE (f. by Cozzene). 9 wins, 3 to 5, $522,455, Arlington
    Matron H. **[G3]**, Modesty H. **[G3]**, Oaklawn Breeders' Cup H. [L] (OP,
    $94,350), Oklahoma Classics Day Distaff S. [R] (RP, $57,300), Sundance
    S. [L] (LS, $30,000), Oklahoma Classics Day Distaff S. [R] (RP, $28,350),
    2nd Bel Air S. [R] (OP, $10,000), 3rd Three Chimneys Sprinter S. **[G1]**,
    Lady Remington Breeders' Cup S. (RP, $5,425).
  QUACKERBELL (g. by Quack). 5 wins, 2 to 5, $111,918, Blue Ribbon
    Classic Laddie Futurity [L] (BRD, $43,353), Heritage Place Derby [R]
    (RP, $39,378), 2nd Blue Ribbon Classic Derby [R] (BRD, $6,987). Set ntr.

5

6

3rd dam
Cherished Moment, by Graustark. 4 wins at 2 and 3, $56,755, 2nd
    Ashland S.-**G3**. Dam of 6 winners, including--
  One Moment Please. 7 wins at 3 and 5, $99,898.
  Sunset Cloud. 2 wins at 3, $52,575. Producer.
  Summer Paradise. Unraced. Dam of 3 winners, including--
  GAYLA'S PLEASURE. 4 wins at 3, $79,212, Dixie Miss S. (LAD,
    $24,000), 3rd Coca-Cola Fair Grounds Oaks **[G3]**. Producer.

7

14

10

4th dam
PUMPKIN PATCH, by Bold Ruler. Unraced. Half-sister to **HAIL THE PIRATES**
    (sire), **CANDALITA** (dam of **OLYMPIC CIRCUIT**; granddam of
    APPLE CURRENT **[G3]**; etc.), **Full Curl**. Dam of 6 foals to race,
    all winners, including--
  Cherished Moment. Black type-placed winner, see above.
  Judge Mauck. 4 wins, 2 to 4, $46,876, 2nd Lakefront H. Sire.
  Precious Pumpkin. Winner at 3, $8,033. Dam of 5 winners, including--
  SHE'S ALWAYS RIGHT. 4 wins, 2 to 4, $69,763, Joan Alhadeff Lassies
    S. (YM, $31,185).
  Bunch of Smiles. Unraced. Producer. Granddam of **MIRACLE METS** (3 wins
    to 3, placed at 4, 2001, $44,080), **Proud Sunset** (4 wins, $100,405).

Breeders' Cup nominated. ← **9**
Registered New York-bred. ← **8**

5-01

Funny Cide's yearling catalog page.

ANNE M. EBERHARDT

Some farms offer breaking and training.

before you resell it. Not only will your purchase undergo breaking and training, it also will be breezed a short distance for potential buyers before being resold as a two-year-old.

Finding a well-conformed yearling is a must because its pedigree won't be worth much if the yearling turns out to have a flaw that impedes its running style or if the youngster turns up unsound during breaking and training. So, again, be sure to seek the help of an adviser when choosing a yearling to pinhook as a two-year-old; it could mean the difference between success and failure.

A majority of pinhookers who buy yearlings to sell as two-year-olds are based in Florida, where these youngsters can be broken and trained through the winter months to be sold at one of the state's many two-year-old sales. Central Florida, Ocala in particular, is a haven for the breaking and training of young horses. Several

reputable farms in the area offer these services (ranging between $25 and $65 a day), as well as farms in many other parts of the country, primarily Texas, California, Louisiana, South Carolina, and Maryland. Most pinhookers ship their yearlings to someone else for breaking and training. Although some pinhookers run their own breaking and training operations, a newcomer should not undertake this task because of the expertise necessary. Good breaking and training lay the groundwork for a successful racing career, and you should be sure to find a reputable farm to do the job.

The very gradual and gentle process of breaking and training begins fairly quickly for yearlings that will be sold as two-year-olds in training. The juvenile sale season starts as early as February, though some pinhookers wait to sell their two-year-olds until later in the season when they are more physically mature.

Some farms offer sales preparation and management in addition to breaking and training while some just offer breaking and training. Either way, farm management often will work with pinhookers to determine which sale would be most advantageous for their horses. If a farm does not offer sales preparation, it is good to work with a consignor who can offer sales advice and preparation services. Consignors and farm managers also know the ropes and often can help secure better placement in a sale, in addition to helping you determine the right sale.

Most two-year-old sales offer prospective buyers an opportunity to preview the horses breezing. Ones that perform well draw a lot of attention and higher bids while youngsters that display poor form or slow works will fail to attract much interest.

Advantages: Finding a well-conformed yearling with a good pedigree that turns out to be a runner can reap substantial financial rewards. As mentioned earlier, pinhookers averaged an 82 percent rate of return in 2005 on yearlings pinhooked as two-year-olds. This rate of return is pulled up markedly by the super-successful pinhooks — such as Florida horsemen Tony Bowling and Bobby Dodd buying Barbados (Forestry—Rare Bird) as a yearling for $200,000 at the 2004 Fasig-Tipton Kentucky select yearling sale in July and then selling him the following March for $3 million at the 2005 Fasig-Tipton Florida select two-year-olds-in-training sale. In addition to poten-

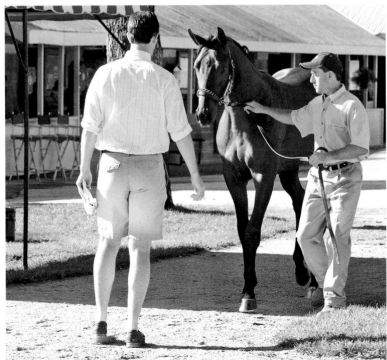

ANNE M. EBERHARDT

Finding a well-conformed yearling with a good pedigree can reap rewards.

ANNE M. EBERHARDT

Good pedigrees are important in broodmare prospects.

tially making money, a pinhooker also can realize many personal rewards such as seeing a youngster grow into a racehorse under his or her watch. All two-year-olds seem full of promise.

Disadvantages: Pinhooking yearlings to two-year-olds is a risky business because of myriad opportunities for things to go wrong — a horse can get injured during breaking and training; a horse might be over-trained in an effort to get it into top shape for a sale, resulting in injury; or the horse might not be a runner, a fact that can't be hidden from potential buyers who watch the horse work before a sale. Buyers also will shy away from horses that show any conformational weaknesses.

Broodmare Prospect to Broodmare

How to: Broodmare prospects — mares that have not yet been bred — are usually purchased at auctions, privately, or off the racetrack in claiming races. They are then bred between February and June and sold in foal at auction later in the year or early the next year.

The easiest way to find a broodmare prospect is through auctions, where large numbers of mares are brought together in one place, and you easily can compare their conformation and temperament.

Most broodmares and broodmare prospects are sold at breeding stock and mixed sales, which take place October through February. The major auction companies are Keeneland and Fasig-Tipton, both with offices in Kentucky, but there are also many regional sales that vary in size and quality.

Claiming a mare as a potential broodmare is more complex and risky, but it offers the chance to make some money if you can claim a good mare at a low price. All horses entered in claiming races are for sale to eligible buyers for a price stated in the program. Rules on who is eligible to claim a horse vary from track to track, so you might need a licensed horseman to make the claim for you.

Claiming prices range from $5,000 to $150,000, and claiming races comprise a majority of the races run in the United States every year. Entries come out two or three days before each claiming race, allowing you time to research the entrants and their pedigrees. But you won't be able to have your veterinarian check out any prospects unless you go to the trainer and ask, thereby communicating your intent to claim the horse. Many horses are placed in claiming races not because their owners want to get rid of them but because they are not good enough to compete in allowance or stakes races. If the trainer wants to hold onto the mare or filly you have inquired after, he or she might withdraw the horse from the race.

Pinhookers who get into buying broodmare prospects want to make sure that they choose horses with good pedigrees, worthy race records, or families known for producing runners. It's not usually a good idea to buy a cheap, unproven mare with a poor pedigree and breed her to an expensive stallion in the hopes of reaping a financial reward at resale. Chances are that among the cost of the mare, the stud fee, the upkeep, and the additional vet bills to ensure and maintain a healthy pregnancy, the pinhooker stands a good chance of losing money. Buying a broodmare prospect with merit and selecting a stallion whose stud fee does not exceed one-third of the broodmare's worth is a much better plan.

Pinhooking potential broodmares requires a lot of work and expense. First, the candidates must be inspected not only for their physical conformation but also for their reproductive conformation. Reproductive conformation refers specifically to whether a vulva is vertical or tipped back. If it is tipped back, the mare will be vulnerable to reproductive tract infections, making it difficult for the mare to get pregnant or carry a foal to term. These mares often can be managed with a surgical stitch known as a Caslick's, but they are still considered high risk. Also, the buyer is taking a chance on a mare that has never been bred, leaving the questions: Will she be able to get pregnant? Will she be able to hold on to that pregnancy? A broodmare prospect that cannot get in foal, has difficulty holding on to a pregnancy, or requires constant veterinary care will end up costing the buyer money.

If you decide you want to pinhook a potential broodmare, you'll need a safe place to board her or your own farm with veterinary services nearby. You'll want to breed the mare as early in the season as possible. This makes her more attractive to potential buyers, who would like as much time as possible to breed her back after she foals. Also, should the buyer want to sell the resulting weanling instead of keeping it to race, the youngster will be older

ANNE M. EBERHARDT

Buying a broodmare, then selling the resulting weanling can be rewarding.

and more developed when sale time rolls around.

Selecting the right stallion for the task requires some pedigree and conformation expertise and a dose of realism. The idea is to get the most bang for the buck, so choose carefully. As stated earlier, a general rule of thumb is not to spend more than one-third of the broodmare's value on a stud fee. It's also advisable not to spend less than a quarter of the stud fee and run the risk of under-breeding.

Once a stallion is chosen and a contract negotiated with the stallion manager (this is usually done by the fall for the following breeding season), it is your responsibility to transport the mare to the stal-

lion for breeding and to manage her reproductive health (i.e., working with a veterinarian to know her heat cycle and to ensure she is pregnant). This is a time- and energy-intensive venture unless someone else is hired to manage the broodmare's breeding, adding to the expense. The mare may have to be bred back more than once and managed carefully by a veterinarian to get pregnant or she may conceive right away.

Once the mare is pregnant, veterinary care is necessary to make sure she maintains a healthy pregnancy, again adding to the cost of upkeep.

Most broodmares are sold at mixed sales. An adviser or broodmare farm manager can help determine the proper sale and help you prepare the broodmare for resale.

Advantages: If you are looking for a very active, hands-on pinhooking experience, this might be the right fit. A lot of management is required, from choosing the mare to selecting a stallion to monitoring the mare's heat cycles to ensuring conception and a healthy pregnancy.

Disadvantages: This is probably pinhooking at its riskiest without the likelihood of a substantial reward. More than 50 percent of broodmares in 2005 sold for $10,000 or less, making profitability a tough prospect. There is also the opportunity for things to go wrong with an unproven mare: She may be barren or she may need close management to get in foal and stay in foal. All of this can cost you a lot of money.

Broodmare to Broodmare

How to: Buying a broodmare, selling the resulting weanling, and then breeding back the broodmare and selling her in foal also is a very intensive pinhooking effort. You face many of the same issues mentioned in the previous section but have the additional expense, energy, and risk of foaling and ensuring the broodmare stays in good reproductive health to be bred back as quickly as possible.

Having a broodmare in sound breeding condition is important because mares are not the most reproductively efficient animals in the world. Age also is a factor. Over time, producing foals causes wear and tear on the reproductive sys-

tem, especially the uterus. So age is one consideration when initially selecting a broodmare.

Of course, a broodmare's produce record is of utmost importance. Were there years she was barren? Whom has she been bred to previously? Does she have progeny that are already racing? How are they faring? Whom is she currently in foal to and how has this stallion fared as a sire? Does he have any progeny of note? What have been the results of mixing these family lines? How popular are these family lines? These are questions best discussed with an adviser before picking out a broodmare.

You can either board a broodmare on a farm that specializes in taking care of pregnant horses, the resulting foals, and getting the mares back in foal; or if you have a farm with a safe area for the mother, and the foal that will join her, she can be kept there, provided you have good veterinary care and experienced guidance. Ideally, about thirty to forty-five days before she is due, a broodmare should be brought nightly inside the stall in which she will foal so that she can get used to the surroundings and feel safe. She must also build up immunity to any pathogens in the surroundings so that she can pass immunity on to her foal in her colostrum (first milk). The field in which she is turned out also must be kept cleared of manure in case she foals in the field, a situation that is fine provided the weather is not too cold. Again, it is important that she and her foal be safe from other horses. It is also imperative to have someone who is experienced with foaling to recognize labor, help with the process, and know when something is not going right so that a veterinarian can be summoned. This is not an undertaking for a novice.

The mare, hopefully, can be bred back quickly, but her heat cycles need to be managed for optimum timing. Again, this requires knowledge or you working closely with a veterinarian to make sure the mare is ready when she is sent for breeding. If all goes well, the pregnancy will take and the broodmare can be sold at the same sale as the weanling, or they can be sold at different sales, depending on the circumstances.

Advantages: Again, this type of pinhooking is good if you want to make a lot of decisions and enjoy breeding and foaling. Watching a foal come into the world can be a spectacular experience. If done at the higher financial levels, this type of pinhooking can be very lucrative. The 2005 sales in North America yielded twenty-nine broodmares that sold for a million dollars or more.

Disadvantages: This endeavor needs to be very tightly managed because of its seasonal nature and because of all the decisions that must be made. It has the potential to become very expensive with veterinary bills, boarding costs, stud fees, transportation costs, etc., without the guarantee of recouping those costs, let alone making a profit.   — *Rena Baer*

Preparing a Business Plan

Pinhooking has the same allure as any other speculative investment, an enticing opportunity to buy low, sell high, and turn a quick profit. Pinhooking and investing also share similar risks. You might misjudge the market and pay too much, winding up with a horse that you can't resell for a profit. Or you might make a shrewd buy only to have the horse suffer an injury or become ill. Or the expenses associated with getting your purchase back in front of potential buyers turn out to be more than you expected and a sea of red ink replaces the anticipated profit.

You cannot eliminate missteps in judgment or bad luck; they're part of the game. But they are aspects of your business that you ignore at your own peril. You should try and minimize their effects on your pinhooking business. One way to accomplish that is by doing your homework. Before making your first bid, you should have in place a sound and comprehensive business plan to help maximize your successes and take some of the sting out of the inevitable mistakes or misfortune.

Before proceeding further, you should understand what a business plan is and what it is not. Telling a few friends that you're going to buy a couple of yearlings and resell them as two-year-olds to improve your cash flow isn't a business plan. It's wishful thinking, which isn't necessarily a bad thing. Wishful thinking got you interested in racing in the first place, after all, and your success as a pinhooker depends to a large extent on your customers having a large measure of it as well.

Wishful thinking has no place in a business plan, however. Your business plan should be a realistic assessment of your goals, along with an objective and detailed outline of how you are going to attain them.

Nor should the actual process that you use to decide that Hip No. 231 has potential but that Hip No. 400 doesn't deserve a second look be a part of your business plan. Though vital to your success, those kinds of decisions are too fact-specific to anticipate with any degree of reliability. Your business plan should address your general business philosophy. Do you plan to put all your eggs in one figurative basket by buying one or two expensive weanlings or yearlings for resale and hope for a big score, or do you expect to purchase several lower-priced horses and emphasize quantity over quality?

A well-drafted business plan doesn't dictate every decision, nor should it. Instead, think of your business plan as a road map with the main routes and hazards well-marked, but with sufficient flexibility to allow for a few hopefully pleasant side trips.

Your business plan should

include, at a minimum, the following:
• How the business will be owned;
• How the business will be financed;
• What the projected income and expenses are;
• What tax considerations are involved.

Ownership and Financing

The first decision in your business plan should relate to ownership — will you serve as the only owner or will other people be involved? If the latter, will the business be structured as a partnership or as a corporation? If you set up a partnership will there be only general partners, or a mix of general and limited partners? If you choose the corporate route, will your business be a "C" corporation or an "S" corporation? Or will a limited liability company (LLC), a relatively recent creation of state law, best serve your interests?

It's not an easy decision, nor should it be made without consideration of a number of factors. As we'll see, the type of ownership you choose is closely related to how the business will be financed. Often, the need for financing will dictate the type of ownership. Other possible considerations include your management style, your willingness to share control and decision-making, the choice to assume sole liability for business debts or to spread the risk among other people, and tax issues.

Sole Proprietorship

A sole proprietorship is what its name implies, a business owned and operated by a single individual. It is the simplest way to operate a business, and by far the most common. There are few, if any, legal requirements for establishing a sole proprietorship beyond setting up shop and announcing to the world you're in business. It would be prudent, however, to determine if the name of the business must be registered with state or local authorities in your jurisdiction.

A sole proprietorship is an attractive option for an individual who wants to call all the shots for the business because total control of the operation rests in the hands of the owner. As the sole proprietor, you own all the assets of the business and you can take full credit for all your successes, but you also shoulder all the blame for your mistakes. Profits if you're lucky, or losses if you're not, are reported on the sole proprietor's individual federal and state tax returns.

Concomitant with complete control over the operation of the business is sole liability for all the debts it incurs. Depending on the level of your involvement and your pinhooking skills, those debts can be substantial. Keep in mind that by establishing a sole proprietorship you are putting your personal assets on the line if business assets are not sufficient to cover the debt.

The assets of a business are at risk no matter what ownership structure is selected. Some ownership structures protect an owner's personal assets; some do not. Because a sole proprietor *is* the business, no practical distinction exists between business and personal assets for a one-owner operation.

The ultimate effect of this is that a creditor who obtains a court judgment against a sole proprietor can attack both the assets of the business (such as horses, tack and other equipment, a horse van) and the personal assets of the business owner (such as a house, an automobile, personal property, and personal bank accounts) to satisfy a business debt. This realization can come as a very unpleasant surprise to a sole owner who doesn't understand the ramifications of setting out on his or her own.

Small businesses often fail because the owner or owners lack sufficient start-up capital to weather unexpected expenses or a few bad breaks. Your pinhooking venture is no different. If it is undercapitalized, you will be forced to succeed from the start to maintain a sufficient cash flow to stay afloat. Otherwise, the business inevitably will fail. One of the main benefits of a comprehensive business plan is that it allows you to estimate with a high degree of certainty the amount of capital needed to keep your pinhooking operation going in the face of some early mistakes.

Putting together sufficient start-up financing can be a problem for a sole proprietor, whose access to capital necessarily will be limited to his or her own money or to funds that can be borrowed from other family members or from friends. Bank loans and credit cards may be alternative sources of financing, but neither is an attractive option. Banks are notoriously reluctant to risk money for horse ventures and almost certainly will require personal guarantees for any loans. Cash advances from credit cards should be avoided except in the direst of emergencies because of the high interest rates that accompany them.

A home equity loan or line of

> ## THINGS TO KNOW
>
> Business financing generally comes from one of two sources: lenders or investors. Lenders, such as banks and credit unions, loan business owners money at a fixed interest rate. Profit for the lender comes from the interest paid by the borrower, not directly from the success of the business, although lenders recognize that a successful business owner is far more likely than the owner of a failed business to pay off a loan. Lenders typically have no involvement in management of the business. Investors, on the other hand, generally supply money in return for an ownership interest in the business. The investor's profit is tied directly to the success of the business and an investor may want, expect, or demand an active role in management.

credit also is a possible source of financing for your business. Most lenders offer attractive interest rates for these loans, primarily because the borrower is putting up his or her house as collateral. Defaulting on a home equity loan puts your house at risk of foreclosure.

General Partnership

A partnership is formed when two or more individuals come together to operate an unincorporated business for a profit. Implied in the formation of a partnership is an ongoing business relationship. If two or more individuals join forces for a single business transaction, such as pinhooking only one yearling for resale as a juvenile, the business entity formed is technically not a partnership but a joint venture. Both partnerships and joint ventures are treated the same by the Internal Revenue Service, which allows profits and losses to pass through the business for reporting on each partner's individual tax return. The partnership itself does not pay federal income tax although an informational return must be filed annually.

Establishing a general partnership should be no more complicated than setting up a sole proprietorship. Most states allow but do not require the filing of a partnership agreement, and there are none of the reporting obligations imposed on corporations. Local registration of the business name may or may not be necessary.

Each partner contributes something to the business, either capital, services, expertise, or some combination of the three. Unless there is a written partnership agreement to the contrary, the general partners share equally in the management of the business. The partners also share the profits and losses equally.

Adding partners increases the operating capital of the business, either directly through contributions of money by the partners or indirectly through the contribution of services such as training, boarding, or veterinary care. It is important to match the contributions to the nature of the business, however.

A partner who is more comfortable spending money on several modestly priced yearlings will be a poor fit when the business plan is to purchase one expensive yearling at a time. By the same token, a trainer whose expertise is breaking yearlings and training juveniles might have little to offer a pinhooking partnership with plans to buy weanlings. A business plan provides direction for the operation and gives potential partners insight into what they can expect from the partnership.

General partners share equally in the decision-making and management of the business. If you're uncomfortable sharing these responsibilities with others, a sole proprietorship may be a better choice despite the possibly reduced access to operating capital.

General partners also have joint and several liability for all debts incurred by the business. This means that each partner is legally responsible for *all* the debts of the partnership. A creditor can proceed in court against all the partners, against some of the partners, or

THINGS TO KNOW

A partnership agreement is the legal contract that establishes the business and sets out the rights and obligations of the partners. A written agreement usually is not a legal requirement for a general partnership, but a partnership agreement should be in writing to avoid any disputes over the terms of the agreement. A written agreement is a necessity for limited partnerships due to the limitations on the partners' liability for business debts. If a dispute arises over an unwritten general partnership agreement, a court often will resolve the dispute by reference to the Uniform Partnership Act. The UPA has been adopted in nearly all jurisdictions and provides a legally sound default agreement for business partnerships set up without anything on paper. It also is not uncommon for general partnerships to borrow language found in the UPA for their written agreements.

ANNE M. EBERHARDT

W. Cothran Campbell (center) is a pioneer of racing partnerships.

against only one individual. As with a sole proprietorship, general partners have no protection for their personal assets, a circumstance that should encourage you to know and trust your business partners.

Limited Partnership

Dogwood Stable owner W. Cothran Campbell popularized limited partnerships in the 1970s as a way to involve people in the ownership of Thoroughbreds while limiting the new owners' economic risks. Campbell would buy a horse, usually a yearling, then offer limited partnership shares in the horse. He would serve as the general partner, making all management decisions for each partnership, while the limited partners essentially went along for the ride.

A limited partnership must include at least one general partner who is responsible for management of the business and who is liable for business debts. The remaining partners can be other general partners, limited partners, or a combination of the two. If there is more than one general partner, they collectively share management responsibility and are jointly and severally liable for business debts.

Limited partners, on the other hand, have no role in decision-making and their potential liability for business debts is limited to the amount of their investment. The personal assets of limited partners thus are not at risk. If a limited partner does become actively involved in management of the partnership, however, the status as a limited partner, along with protection for personal assets, generally is lost.

Limited partnerships can be an effective way to raise capital without surrendering control of the business, but there are potential drawbacks for both the general partner and the limited partners. A limited partnership agreement must be drafted carefully to avoid violating the regulations of the Securities and Exchange Commission and many of the federal income tax breaks once enjoyed by limited partners have been reduced or eliminated.

Corporation

At the mention of the word "corporation," most people conjure up images of General Motors, Exxon, and the New York Stock Exchange. In fact, however, a corporation is any business entity organized under the laws of a state that is separate and distinct from its owners (called shareholders). Establishing a corporation is a complex legal procedure requiring preparation and filing with your state Articles of Incorporation and By Laws for the business. There also are ongoing reporting and record-keeping requirements that must be satisfied to maintain the corporate status. The assistance of an attorney familiar with federal and state filing and reporting requirements will facilitate the process and is highly recommended.

Because a corporation has a separate legal identity, unlike a sole proprietorship or a general partnership, the shareholders do not assume any liability for business debts beyond the value of their investment in company stock. The most a shareholder in a corporation can lose is the amount he or she has invested. Corporate shareholders, like limited partners, enjoy limited liability for business debts.

The separate legal identity also means that the business is obligated to pay federal and state income taxes on business profits at the corporate level. If any of the remaining profits are distributed to the shareholders in the form of divi-

dends, the dividends are reported on the shareholders' individual tax returns and taxed. This results in double taxation, a situation that may or may not be a problem for the shareholders, depending on whether corporate or individual tax rates are lower.

An exception to the double taxation scheme results if the corporation is organized under Subchapter S of the tax code. While large corporations must be set up under Subchapter C, hence the name "C" corporation, an "S" corporation has a limited number of shareholders. If certain other requirements are satisfied, an S corporation may elect to avoid the corporate tax and have profits taxed directly to the shareholders.

Incorporating your pinhooking business provides protection for your personal assets and theoretically, at least, is a viable way to bring investors and their capital into the business. Because of the complicated filing and reporting procedures, however, there almost certainly are other similar and equally effective ways to accomplish the same things.

Limited Liability Company

A limited liability company (LLC) may be the best of all possible worlds when starting a new business. Governed by the laws of the state in which it is established, an LLC protects the personal assets of the owners (called "members" rather than partners or shareholders) without the elaborate registration and reporting requirements of a corporation. Also unlike a corporation, an LLC is not a separate legal entity apart from the owners and the double taxation problem of a C corporation can be avoided.

In summary, the ownership structure you choose for your business will be dictated by several factors, the most important of which may be the need for outside financing and the desire to protect your personal assets. A sole proprietorship restricts your access to financing and neither that option nor a general partnership protects your personal assets. Of the choices that limit your personal liability for business debts, a corporation or limited liability company, an LLC is by far the simpler type of ownership.

Income and Expenses

The essence of pinhooking is reselling a horse for more than the original purchase price to show a profit. The concept sounds simple, and it can be — if you know how much the pinhooked horse must bring on resale to cover *all* your expenses. Without knowing how much money you've really got in the horse, it is impossible to put a realistic price on the animal.

Keep in mind that the original purchase price is only one of many expenses associated with getting a horse back in the sale ring or in front of a private buyer. A $50,000 yearling resold as a two-year-old in training for $100,000 might be a profitable transaction, or it might not be, depending upon your other expenses.

The risk of loss passes from the seller to the buyer at the fall of the auctioneer's hammer, and you may want to insure the animal at that point. There will be boarding expenses, breaking and training bills (if you're planning on reselling the horse as a two-year-old in training), veterinary care, farrier services, transportation costs, advertising, fees for sales

> **THINGS TO KNOW**
>
> If you choose either a corporation or a limited liability company for your pinhooking business, keep in mind that either "Inc." or "LLC" must follow the name of your business in all communications. This is a legal requirement to put anyone with whom you do business on notice that the personal liability of the owners is limited.

agents if you use them, and sales prep.

There will be interest on loans if you've borrowed money, and fees for accountants and attorneys if you've needed their services. You'll have travel and entertainment expenses and the commission due the sales company. Horses that don't bring as much as you expected on resale may create losses that you must absorb. The list goes on and on, and what seemed like a substantial profit at first can turn into a loss.

At this point your business plan comes into play. You probably cannot know for certain how much you will spend on pinhooked horses during a year because that figure will be determined by the market. You can know how much capital will be available to buy horses and to pay expenses.

If the first-year goal is to buy a single weanling in November for resale as a yearling the following summer or fall, for example, your business plan should include realistic estimates of all the expenses necessary to do that. Subtracting the projected outlay for expenses from the available capital puts a cap on how much you should pay for the weanling. Any amount

ANNE M. EBERHARDT

The buyer should consider insuring the horse.

beyond that may not leave sufficient capital for the business to pay its bills. Spending more money than you've got may work for the government, but it isn't a sound business strategy if you lack the ability to print your own money.

Estimating the total expenses also gives you a good idea of how much the horse must bring on resale to show a profit. If the plan calls for pinhooking several horses, simply multiply the expenses for one horse by the number of horses you intend to buy.

This portion of your business plan can, and should, be revised regularly to reflect changes in ownership, shifts in goals for the operation, purchases of horses or other assets, profits or losses from resales that change the available capital, and unexpected expenses. Your business plan should be flexible enough to accommodate changes in the operation but comprehensive enough to prevent unpleasant sur-

prises when you balance the books after reselling a horse.

Estimates of income and expenses are valuable planning tools for a business owner. They are essential parts of your business plan if you expect to seek outside financing. Commercial lenders and most investors might share your passion for horses and racing, but that passion won't drive their choices. Instead, they will make decisions to lend money or invest in your pinhooking operation on their assessments of your chances for success. They will expect to see familiar things like income/ expense summaries and projected balance sheets in a loan application or a prospectus, and the more businesslike you appear the more likely you are to get a loan or attract investors.

Tax Considerations

Tax planning and business planning go hand in hand in several important ways. First, an effective business plan can be a significant step toward establishing that your pinhooking operation is a business and not a hobby in the eyes of the Internal Revenue Service. This distinction will allow you to use any losses you suffer as a pinhooker to reduce taxable income from other activities, if there are any. No one likes to lose money, but things don't always go as planned for even the best-run operations. Putting the losses to work softens the sting.

If the pinhooking operation is your sole source of income, the business/hobby distinction obviously is less important than if it is one of several revenue-producing activities. If that is the situation, and you are losing money, you won't stay in business.

Second, a well-constructed business plan provides a framework for good record-keeping, which allows you to take all available deductions at tax time. Also, the timing of purchases and sales may be structured to allow the activity to show a profit in a particular year. If your horse activity shows a profit in two out of seven years, the activity is presumed to be a business for federal tax purposes.

Although this is an over-simplification of the actual statutory language, the presumption is one of very few advantages in the tax code enjoyed by the owners of horse operations. Most other activities are presumed to be a business only when there are three profitable years out of five, a more demanding standard.

Congress and state legislatures often work under the misguided impression that anyone involved in the horse business is a wealthy dilettante not deserving of any tax

breaks. The result is that it may become necessary to prove to the IRS that you actually are engaged in a real business. The IRS allows a taxpayer to use losses from one activity to reduce taxable income from other sources but only if the loss-producer is a business and not a hobby. Hobby losses can be deducted only to the extent of income from the activity, which means that while a hobby can lose money, a hobby cannot generate a loss for tax purposes.

In the eyes of the IRS a "business" is an activity undertaken for profit. If the IRS challenges the status of your pinhooking operation, auditors and courts will look at nine tests to determine whether you have a business or a hobby. One of the most important of the tests is whether you conduct the affairs of the activity in a businesslike manner.

Courts repeatedly refer to the use of a sound business plan as one of the indicators of a businesslike activity. Failure to have a business plan or the failure to adapt an existing business plan to improve the financial status of the activity often

> **THINGS**TO**KNOW**
>
> The federal tax code has more than 60,000 pages, and effective tax planning is well beyond the scope of this book. Tax considerations are among the many reasons that your accountant, and possibly your attorney, should be involved throughout the development and implementation of your business plan.

suggests to courts that the activity is really a hobby. Consider, for example, a business plan that calls for boarding your pinhooked weanlings at a very expensive, top-of-the-line facility. If you lose money when the pinhooked horses are resold as yearlings, it might be prudent to review the business plan and switch to a cheaper boarding farm. Staying with a plan that isn't working won't impress the IRS.

Good record-keeping also is an indicator of a well-run operation and your business plan can help with this task. Because you estimated all the probable expenses you are likely to incur when drafting the business plan, you should have a good idea of the record-keeping requirements for the activity. The IRS allows a taxpayer to deduct from gross income all expenses that are reasonable and necessary to the operation of your business. You will be much less likely to overlook deductible expenses if you have a good record-keeping process in place than if you let receipts accumulate in a shoebox under the bed until tax time.

Developing a good business plan is without a doubt a substantial amount of work, without any of the fun and excitement of actually buying and selling horses. It may be tempting to forge ahead without a formal plan, and many successful pinhookers do just that. Planning is never a bad idea, however, especially if you are new to the game, and the time and effort necessary to develop a comprehensive business plan will be time well spent. — *Milton C. Toby*

4

Picking the Right Horse

Searching for the right horse to acquire in a pinhooking venture really begins with a search for the right people.

A team of advisers is considered necessary even for seasoned horsemen who want to compete in a high-risk market some describe as an emotional and financial roller coaster that can take a variety of plunges on the way to anticipated peaks.

Depending on the type of venture, the professional advisers that should be considered before thoughts of bidding at sales are entertained include bankers, lawyers, accountants, insurance agents, bloodstock agents, trainers, and veterinarians.

Joel Turner, an equine-law specialist with the firm of Frost Brown Todd in Louisville, Kentucky, and an owner, breeder, and pinhooker himself, stresses that a vetting process must begin with the people.

"The most important thing is to check references; do some due diligence. Don't just take a referral and say, 'Well, he's a good guy,' " Turner said.

Investors also should set realistic goals and seek to align themselves with professionals who can help them reach those aspirations.

"If the primary focus is business, then they should slowly and deliberately assemble a small team of people known within the horse industry to possess both experience backed by proof of success and high ethical standards," said veterinarian Dr. Jeff Berk of Ocala Equine Hospital in Ocala, Florida, who often conducts presale examinations of young horses for clients and who helped draft the American Association of Equine Practitioners' recommended rules on medication use in horses at public auctions. "They should rely on the input of this team and immerse themselves in the process while learning."

A legal adviser can recommend what kind of business structure would work best regarding both the investment and liability protection angles.

"The legal issues come up when relative newcomers say, 'This looks like an easy game. There's a big gap between yearling prices and two-year-old prices and there is the potential for profit,' " Turner noted. Some pinhooking deals that may seem like partnerships actually can be subject to securities laws, as are stocks. If these arrangements "don't comply fully and they lose money and somebody is really unhappy, I believe there is a lot of [negative] exposure" for organizers, he said.

If investors go into pinhooking in their individual names, they also risk exposing themselves to liability they could at least partly shield themselves from by forming a limited liability company or a Subchapter S or Subchapter C cor-

35

poration, depending on the size of the venture.

To cover another risk, mortality insurance is available for the horses purchased, but Turner points out that there is really no cost effectively way to insure for injury or loss of use.

Legal, financial, and fiduciary considerations are critical even for experienced horsemen, advises Becky Thomas of Sequel Bloodstock, who has pinhooked horses for two decades. "Being a good horseman is not the end all — you can't survive without all those elements going into play," she said.

Planning should include financial projections and setting aside enough reserves to pay expenses between the time of purchase and the time of sale, factoring in the possibility that each horse may not be ready for a targeted sale due to illness or other setbacks.

After these business aspects are addressed, the focus can shift to associating with professionals such as bloodstock agents and veterinarians who rate horses and their profit potential prior to purchase.

Most buyers develop longstanding working relationships with their veterinarians, and they rely on their combined experiences regarding horses they have considered or bought in the past while making assessments of new prospects.

"You must be on the same page as your veterinarian," said Thomas, who annually spends about $5 million on horses, including breeding stock as well as her pinhooks of young horses.

"The importance of the veterinarian in the process of selecting horses is determined by each individual veterinarian's ability to

Becky Thomas of Sequel Bloodstock

properly interpret veterinary findings and assign them their respective risk factors," Berk explained. "It is possible to err on one side or the other, either by placing too much emphasis on findings that may be nothing more than a variation of normal or underestimating the importance of a subtle finding in a high-risk location. A veterinarian that is able to sort through these issues properly can be very valuable to a buyer.

"Each buyer has a different comfort level with the risk inherent in the unique veterinary findings in each individual horse," he added.

With weanlings or yearlings being pinhooked for sale as yearlings or two-year-olds, respectively, Berk says the exams he performs for clients involve primarily endoscopic views of airways — aimed at detecting any restrictions — and reviews of radiographs of front and hind fetlocks as well as knees, stifles, and hocks. Clients factor in his opinions with their own views of individuals' conformation and movement to determine a horse's suitability for their program.

Often in today's pinhooking world, where prices have skyrocketed for the best horses, buyers have to group together to have enough capital to play the game effectively. Spreading risk by buying at least six to ten horses annually can be critical for business ventures, Turner says.

Bloodstock agents such as Mike Ryan have formed separate entities in which many investors can participate along with the organizers; Ryan and his business partner, consignor and trainer Niall Brennan, have their own money at stake along with that of the people with whom they partner. Called Top Yield Bloodstock, the Ryan-Brennan operation gives pinhooking investors an inside look at the business; financial returns since 1993 are posted on its Web site. Those results show the potential and the risk, with distributions per

investment unit varying from less than a chilling –20 percent to more than a sizzling 110 percent, with all but one year showing a profit.

Top Yield has a core of 40 to 50 investors who participate in partnerships formed annually when new horses are acquired for resale, Brennan notes.

Thomas, who began her pinhooking business in 1986 on the strength of a $10,000 loan, seeks an overall return of about 15 percent to 20 percent. Although she sold 394 juveniles for more than $62 million between 1996 and 2005, she candidly advises that people shouldn't try pinhooking

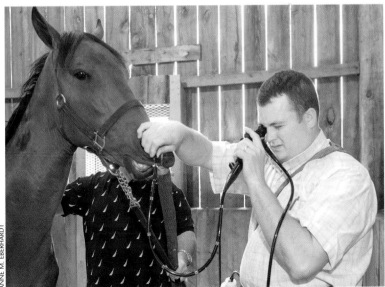

It's important to enlist the services of a veterinarian when buying prospects.

Have the veterinarian review all pertinent X-rays.

ALEXANDER BARKOFF

unless they are prepared to lose all their money — and possibly more.

"The risk can be much higher than the reward," she said, pointing to the chance of pre-sale training injuries that can eliminate promising horses from generating any return. "I don't recommend it for the faint of heart. Euphoria can quickly turn to a terrible depression."

Choosing the Venue for Purchase

Judging from information and statistics he has gathered during his experience in the business, Turner said that only about one in four horses generally makes a prof-

it for pinhookers, considering the expenses involved; however, others have pegged the profit rate higher, estimating that about half of pinhooked horses are profitable. The fact that a large percentage of pinhooks are not profitable dramatically underlines the importance of a savvy bloodstock agent in selecting horses for pinhooking ventures. Brennan and Thomas, who has taken on only a few minority partners in her business over the years, both say it is necessary to search all major yearling sales and some regional sales for prospects.

Two yearling sales important to pinhookers are the Keeneland September venue, which, as the world's largest, offers something for every buyer, and the Fasig-Tipton July sale, which emphasizes progeny of young sires.

Inspecting as many horses as possible at the sales is paramount. In pinhooking, conformation and presence of the individual are the

---

THINGSTO**KNOW**

At the sales, inspecting as many horses as possible is paramount. In pinhooking, conformation, presence, and athleticism of the individual are the most essential elements. Pedigree is secondary except as a guide to cost.

---

most essential elements; pedigree is secondary except as a guideline to cost. Horses with both exceptional conformation and pedigree often are too expensive to justify the risk.

"The first priority is the individual, the conformation, the athleticism," Brennan stated. "If we find a horse that we love physically and he's got a tremendous pedigree, we automatically know he's probably going to be well out of our price range."

her mind and not bid at all on a previously well-regarded prospect if she is not impressed with how he is handling himself prior to being led into the sale ring. Unruly, studdish colts are likely to be "ten times worse" as they grow older, she advises. The ability to change a pricing assessment under pressure can separate successful pinhookers from their colleagues, but if a budget is surpassed on one horse, it must be regained somewhere else.

It's important for pinhookers to inspect as many horses as possible at a sale.

Thomas says her key criterion is a well-balanced individual.

"You can look at a horse that has a lot of parts that are really nice, but if they don't all fit together, the whole picture doesn't work for me. I can forgive a multitude of sins if the package is there," she said.

She also considers a horse's demeanor and manners, rejecting those that exhibit problematic quirks and adjusting her pricing assessments when warranted. For example, she said she has changed

As Thomas notes, "the goal is to make money," and there will always be some desired horses that could not be obtained.

"With hindsight, there are lots of horses I wish I had bought," Thomas said, "but there are lots more I'm glad I didn't buy."

Diversifying the pinhooking portfolio is a key consideration when selecting horses. Acquisitions ideally should span a variety of foaling dates to avoid a glut of younger individuals that might not sell as well as more mature members of the same generation, Turner, the equine-law specialist, says.

Additionally, pinhooked individuals must offer what the resale market demands. Horses that have been preferred at recent auctions favored by pinhookers include those by successful juvenile sires, those with young sires who had early racetrack success themselves, and those out of young mares from precocious families. Of course, individuals with excellent pedigrees and conformation will sell well in any market.

Pinhookers should study trends of successful sires in various sectors

and other relevant data provided by specialized industry publications such as *The Blood-Horse MarketWatch* newsletter, Turner and Thomas note.

Once the horses are purchased, the next step is development. With yearlings, this phase includes breaking and training, processes that naturally raise the risk of injury as physical activity increases. The talents of the trainer involved in the yearling-to-two-year-old pinhooks become an essential ingredient at this stage.

"Keeping the two-year-olds happy is very, very important," said Brennan, who relishes the

Keeping two-year-olds happy helps with their development.

LOUISE E. REINAGEL

ANNE M. EBERHARDT

Niall Brennan, a consignor and trainer.

thrill of schooling youngsters that could turn out "to be the next Secretariat.

"If they're not happy, I want to know the reason, either mentally or physically, and you need to back off and realize that this horse is not ready for this stress at this time. If you don't, you're not going to have a horse left to sell. To be successful, the horse has to come number one. If you know your horse, you're going to do a good job because you're going to let the horse tell you what he can do."

Choosing the Venue for Sale

During training, pinhookers must choose the venue at which to resell each individual, which is one of the most challenging aspects of pinhooking. Although consignors often want to sell early in the season to generate cash flow, they might be better off waiting with some individuals that could flourish with more time.

"You can't make a horse fit a sale; you have to make the sale fit the horse," Brennan said, adding that he nominates each individual to two or three venues for options. "Being in the right place at the right time is why horses sell well. And you've got to help them peak on the right day."

Thomas also tries to place individuals in sales, depending on their appeal to different markets. For example, she might offer a half sibling to a California Cup winner at a Barrett's sale in that state.

Once horses have emerged from early training unscathed — and, as Turner notes, in today's market young horses must be virtually perfect physically to sell well — then they must breeze rapidly at the sale grounds.

"If you don't breeze well, you're dead," Brennan declared, although he does not believe every horse has to rush through a furlong in approximately :10 to be a good prospect. Nevertheless, that is what the market seems to demand, and even shrewd horsemen may lose interest in a two-year-old if he does not perform well in the sale breeze show.

Pinhookers virtually hold their breaths during this crucial period. If horses breeze and show well, then hope abounds they will generate returns far beyond what could be expected with more traditional investments.

Brennan, who for Top Yield sold a Stephen Got Even colt purchased for $157,000 for a short-lived

THINGS TO KNOW

Horses that pinhookers prefer include those by successful juvenile sires, those by young sires that had early racetrack success themselves, and those out of young mares from precocious families. An individual with excellent pedigree and conformation will sell well in any market.

world record of $3.1-million, warns that despite that kind of spectacular result, "pinhooking is a tough game. It's all or nothing. You take your lumps with your gravy.

"Each year it's gotten tougher," he added. "The relative numbers of the horses sold have decreased, and that's across the board so we're all affected. Pinhookers often have a decision to make: you either give your horses away at a loss or if you put your money where your mouth is, you do what we do — you go on and train them and hope you can sell them at the racetrack. So all pinhooking endeavors in recent years have inevitably become pinhooking/racing endeavors."

Still, the lure of selling a horse that only cost thousands for millions can be irresistible to those who can afford the risks.

"I don't think I'm very far ahead in the pinhooking game," confided Turner. "But I've enjoyed trying, and you can't hit a home run unless you step up to the plate. You've got to be in there swinging."

— *Michele MacDonald*

5

Keys to Success

The traditional strategy in pinhooking is to buy low and sell high. Some people do make a living — and a very good one — acquiring top prospects, based on conformation and pedigree, for big bucks and then reselling them for even higher prices. But that is an extremely risky venture that can place an investor in financial peril when just one horse suffers an injury, fails to work fast, or doesn't develop into a physically attractive individual.

Most pinhookers look for bargains when they purchase their prospects. And that means they probably will have to sacrifice one or more aspects of conformation and/or pedigree in their selection process to keep the amount they spend low enough to improve their chance to turn a profit.

A popular strategy for pinhooking mares involves claiming runners that have attractive pedigrees but lack impressive racing records. With young horses that have never been to the races, the process is a bit more complicated.

There are no hard and fast rules. But several pinhookers — Headley

The 2006 stakes winner What a Song sold for $95,000 as a yearling and $1.9 million as a two-year-old.

Bell and Marette Farrell of Nicoma Bloodstock in Kentucky and Kentucky bloodstock agent John Moynihan — offered some general suggestions to keep in mind when seeking a diamond in the rough.

Bell and Farrell enjoyed success in 2006 with a pair of two-year-olds: Exhale, a son of Millenium Wind, and a Deputy Commander—Regrets Only colt. They bought Exhale for $100,000 as a yearling and resold him for $800,000 through Florida pinhooker Niall Brennan. They acquired the Deputy Commander colt for $105,000 and resold him for $475,000, also through Brennan.

Bell and Farrell also buy horses to race for their clients and offer advice on matings. Through their various services, they have been associated with such successful runners as 2006 Kentucky Derby Presented by Yum! Brands winner Barbaro, 2005 NetJets Breeders' Cup Mile winner Artie Schiller, 2003 Woodford Reserve Turf Classic Stakes winner Honor in War, 2000 Del Mar Oaks winner No Matter What, European champion Muhtarram, and grade II winner Northern Afleet, the sire of champion Afleet Alex.

Moynihan also buys pinhooking prospects and horses to race for his clients, who have included wine mogul Jess Jackson and the late Bob Lewis. Moynihan's pinhooking successes include Gotham City. In 1998, the agent advised Martin Cherry to purchase the son of Saint Ballado privately as a weanling. The price was $150,000, according to Jeff Schwietert, whose father, Carl F. Schwietert, bred Gotham City. Two years later the Jerry Bailey Sales Agency resold the colt for $2 million at the Barretts March select sale

of two-year-olds in training.

Moynihan also has been an adviser in the purchases of such horses as 1997 Belmont Stakes winner Touch Gold, 1999 Horse of the Year Charismatic, and grade II winners Exploit and Henny Hughes.

As pinhookers, Bell, Farrell, and Moynihan all face tough tasks. They know buyers are picky and want the equine equivalent of the sun, the moon, and the stars. That package includes outstanding conformation and a black-type pedigree. In a two-year-old, shoppers also want a horse that works fast. The buyers who pay premium prices also want quick colts with bloodlines that contain some stamina and bodies with enough scope (length of body and legs) to suggest that they can win the Kentucky Derby.

Yet, at the same time, Bell, Farrell, Moynihan, and others like them must somehow find the horse that has all those credentials for a price that doesn't suggest it is destined for greatness.

That requires looking at hundreds, sometimes thousands, of horses. It also requires knowledge of numerous factors, including a horse's birth date, the age of its dam, and the physical appearance of other offspring by its sire, dam, and broodmare sire. Some of that information is acquired through years of experience while some can be found in a publication such as Blood-Horse Publication's *Auction Edge*, which contains the pedigrees of horses in a sale and a variety of data about those animals, including auction prices and race records of their family members.

"There are some families that I know that produce yearlings that are kind of small, but by the time they get to the two-year-old level, those horses are normal in size," Moynihan said. "A lot of times you can make some pretty shrewd buys if you know that kind of thing. You see a lot of top horses at the two-year-old sales that when you go back and look at why they were inexpensive as yearlings, it was because they weren't big, mature horses. In between the time the people bought them as yearlings and sold them as two-year-olds, those horses underwent a tremendous amount of growth."

In addition, "I've had great luck buying late foals," Moynihan said. "Touch Gold was a May 26 foal, and Exploit was a May 25 foal. But you have to be careful. When I buy expensive late foals, I make sure their leg conformation is as perfect as perfect can be. Because of their lack of maturity, they can change quite a bit compared to early foals."

In evaluating the conformation of a young horse as a pinhooking prospect, according to Moynihan,

> **THINGS** TO **KNOW**
>
> When evaluating the conformation of a weanling or yearling pinhooking prospect, keep in mind the often dramatic changes that can occur during the various stages of growth. This "eye" develops with time and experience. Therefore, pinhooking novices should seek the advice of reputable and knowledgeable advisers.

you need to keep in mind the rate at which weanlings and yearlings develop and their stages of growth.

"The thing I can't overemphasize is that there can be an unbelievable amount of change conformationally from a weanling to a yearling," he said. "They change in their knee conformation, and they change in the degree of their correctness. The yearlings are pretty much set up. What you see when you're buying a yearling to pinhook as a two-year-old is pretty much what you are going to get."

Weanlings that are "toed out and kind of in at the knee" often will improve in their conformation, Moynihan said. "As their chest broadens, they tend to come around into becoming more correct."

Another key to evaluating a young horse as a pinhooking prospect is understanding what he will be asked to do when he is resold. If you are buying a weanling, how he walks is important because that is how buyers will judge him as a yearling.

"You want a good mover that has a good overstep, which is when the front foot lands in a particular spot, the hind foot will step beyond that," Farrell said.

It is also important that whatever conformation faults the weanling has, they are not so severe that he

ANNE M. EBERHARDT

John Moynihan, a successful pinhooker.

ANNE M. EBERHARDT

Young horses can grow out of conformation flaws. Conversely, flaws can worsen.

can't "walk through" them. What that means, according to Farrell, is that the hind feet and the front basically walk in the same path while the horse is moving forward.

"That shows an economy of motion," she explained, and it means their forward motion is going to be so much better in a race. It's a clean forward movement as opposed to a foot swinging out there because when they gallop, it's going to be even farther out there. A horse can be offset or rotated, but its foot can still land in

THINGSTO**KNOW**

Another key to evaluating a young horse as a pinhooking prospect is to understand what he will be asked to do when he is resold. A weanling's walk is important as yearling buyers will judge him on that basis.

a true straight path."

If you are buying a yearling to resell as a two-year-old, an impressive walk is important, too. But you need to remember that he also will be asked to breeze fast for a short distance and to look athletic while doing it.

"With yearlings, you're going to look at power from behind; that's number one," Farrell said. "They're going to have to go as fast as they can for an eighth of a mile or a quarter mile, so you really want a strong hip, a strong gaskin, a strong hock. You also want good feet and everything moving in a straight line. They also need to have a good shoulder because they will use that shoulder to stretch out and look good on the video (of their workout). They also need a good long neck and some length and scope (in their body)."

In buying horses to pinhook, Moynihan tends to be more forgiving of conformation flaws if a horse is a yearling than if it is a weanling. That's because when the yearling is offered as a two-year-old, buyers at that level often are less critical about faults because the horse has been in training and has shown he can work at speed without being compromised significantly.

"There are horses that I've passed on at the yearling level that I have gone and bought at the two-year-old level," Moynihan said. "When you are at the yearling level, you say, 'Well, this horse is a little upright. He may not move the best, and that is a concern. But if at the two-year-old level you watch that same horse breeze and he moves beautifully, then the worry you had at the yearling sale is probably unwarranted at that point. You can see for yourself that the horse is doing fine."

The severity of a conformation flaw and the build of the horse are other factors Moynihan takes into consideration when deciding whether to buy a horse with a conformation flaw.

"I've had great success buying horses that were a little back at the knee," he said, "but they were slightly made horses. They never carried a lot of weight. They were lean, and they were all beautiful movers. If you buy a horse that is back at the knee and he is this great big heavy thing that hits the ground hard, then you know he will fracture that knee. It will happen. The lean one may fracture his knee, too, but it's a lot less likely."

Moynihan, Bell, and Farrell all mention the importance of balance in selecting a pinhooking prospect. It's a concept that almost every horseman understands, but each uses different words to explain it. Carl Bowling, a Florida-based pinhooker, once offered this definition: "Balance is like a teeter-totter — a plank that has the same weight on both ends. Look at a photograph of a horse from the side. If you could cut off the head and neck and switch them to the other end of the horse, they would look like they belonged there. You don't want a horse with a big front end or no rear end or a horse that has a big hip or a little front end. It should be like a hotdog bun, the same on each end."

In general, Moynihan, Bell, and Farrell agree, it is easier to sacrifice pedigree than conformation when selecting pinhooking prospects.

"Most of my pinhooking successes have been conformation driven," Moynihan said. "If I'm going to the two-year-old sales with a horse to pinhook, conformation is very, very difficult to sacrifice because, in essence, that's what you hope is going to make a horse fast, how it is engineered."

Said Bell: "It all gets back to the individual. It's the number one ingredient, period."

Among the buying strategies used by pinhookers to cut costs from a pedigree standpoint is to buy the offspring from a stallion's first crop. The reasoning is that the horses will be less expensive because their sire has no proven runners. Also, when those horses are resold, the stallion still will have no proven runners, so the chances for a negative reception on the part of buyers are lessened. But that approach has become so popular in recent years that many pinhookers are having trouble finding bargains.

When considering the pedigree of a pinhooking prospect he likes physically, especially that of a yearling he wants to resell as a two-year-old, Moynihan pays particular attention to the produce record of the young horse's dam.

"Sometimes you may have to sacrifice a little on the female side," Moynihan said. "In other words, you buy a first foal or buy a foal out of a mare that really hasn't produced anything successful. If you look up a mare's produce record, and her offspring have brought $20,000, $19,000, and $30,000 RNA (reserve not attained) at auction or earned those amounts, chances are those were not great physical horses. Where a lot of people would look at it and say, 'This mare has never had a runner,' I look at it and say, 'This mare has never had a chance to have a runner. And she probably has never had one that looks like this horse.' A lot of times, you can get great value for a horse like that you are buying, at least in respect to what you have to pay and the cost to get him resold."

Bell and Farrell follow the sire records of stallions. Most horses have cyclical results on the racetrack; sometimes their offspring are hot, and sometimes they are cold.

"We are big on the timing of stallions," Bell said. "We try to anticipate stallions that we think produce racehorses that aren't necessarily hot at the time we are buying and hope that they will be hot when we resell their offspring that we buy."

Often, it works like this. A horse goes to stud, and in his first crop he gets a classic winner or another successful runner. As a result, he gets better mares. Even though he may go cold for a while after that

Good conformation is imperative for Moynihan and other pinhookers.

ANNE M. EBERHARDT

ANNE M. EBERHARDT

Deputy Glitters helped popularize the offspring of Deputy Commander before the 2006 Kentucky Derby.

initial success, he may get hot again when the offspring of those better mares start to race. That's when Bell and Farrell want to be reselling that stallion's progeny.

"When we bought the Deputy Commander colt as a yearling, his sire wasn't necessarily a hot stallion; in fact, he was a cold horse," Bell said. "Yet, when we did our research, we realized that he had more potential runners in 2006 than when he started off and sired Ten Most Wanted. He started off well and then he had gone quiet. But we felt like he might pop up back up again a little bit, and it just so happened we got lucky."

Said Farrell: "Right before that Deputy Commander colt sold (as a two-year-old), Deputy Glitters won the Tampa Bay Derby. And a few other nice horses popped up as well, so it worked. But we also loved that colt as a yearling. He was a beautiful yearling."

With Exhale, Bell and Farrell used the first crop sire strategy, but with a twist. They went with a colt whose sire, Millennium Wind, was overlooked by many buyers and breeders. Millennium Wind won the 2001 Toyota Blue Grass Stakes. His sire, Cryptoclearance, while a success at stud, wasn't very popular commercially. In the group of stallions that entered stud in 2003, Millennium Wind was overshadowed by such sire prospects as Came Home, Orientate, Buddha, Johannesburg, Yonaguska, and Include.

"He (Exhale) was an extraordinary individual, but he was by a first-year sire that wasn't really

THINGS TO KNOW

Among the buying strategies used by pinhookers is to buy the offspring from a stallion's first crop as they generally are less expensive and when they are resold, the stallion will have no runners to influence buyers' decisions.

fashionable," Bell said.

An important pedigree consideration in a yearling being purchased for reselling as a two-year-old is precociousness. Because that yearling will be expected to work fast over a short distance as an early juvenile, you would like him to be by a sire that was a successful racehorse as a two-year-old or has shown that he can produce precocious runners.

"You wouldn't necessarily go look for a horse by a stallion that you know whose offspring perform better later in life and probably at longer distances. But it's a real paradox because you want a horse by a precocious stallion that looks like a classic horse. The real high-ticket horses at two-year-old sales, the ones that usually bring seven figures, the one thing they usually have in common is they all, at least at the time they are sold, demonstrate that they probably aren't limited to sprinting."

Market trends also are factors in pinhooking success. For example, if you resell a horse in a market where the supply of horses is high, it may lower demand. When the Thoroughbred market is on an up cycle, you may be able to sell your pinhooked horses for more money, but you also probably will have to pay more money to acquire them.

The key, in any market, according to Moynihan is to buy horses that you would want to race if you did not resell them. You also need to have the strength to back away when you can't get the horses you want for the prices that you think are reasonable.

"The horses that look like racehorses and that you absolutely love are the ones that you always do well with," Moynihan said. "There are many times when I've tried to buy horses (to pinhook) and I've quit bidding because I said, 'These are just too expensive.' But it's not an exact science. Sometimes you may back off when you shouldn't and sometimes you may buy when you shouldn't. But you've got to do what you are comfortable with."

Bell gave a similar philosophy.

"Even if we are pinhooking a horse, we try to buy what we think will be a racehorse," he said. "Commercial considerations come into it, but we think if you buy what you think is a racehorse to pinhook, then, in the end, the buyers will want that horse."

— *Deirdre B. Biles*

6

Managing the Pinhook Prospect

Once the excitement of buying a young horse to pinhook passes, the pace of business will drop considerably. This slower time is critical, however, particularly for the young horses, the weanling-to-yearling and yearling-to-juvenile pinhooks. It's a time of growth, methodical education, and close observation as the horse matures. Minor adjustments in feeding and training regimens could be worth thousands of dollars down the road. Then as the time to sell approaches, be prepared for a flood of activity and details that will sweep you through the next sale.

Yearling Pinhooks

Life on the farm is particularly slow for weanling-to-yearling pinhooks, which will spend about 85 percent of their days and nights in pastures until nearly two months before an auction. At sixty days out from a sale, the horses begin a conditioning regimen to build muscle.

At Denali Stud, which sells between 200 and 250 yearlings a year, horses are put on an electric walker that works like a large revolving door inside a round pen. Four or five horses simultaneously can walk untethered between the "doors." The speed can be set fast enough that horses can jog while in the

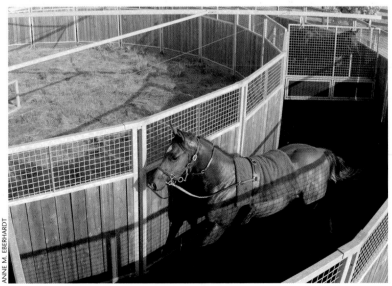

ANNE M. EBERHARDT

A yearling exercising in the electric walker.

walker. The sale horses at Denali might jog on the machine about fifteen to eighteen minutes three or four times a week. Additionally, they are hand-walked twice a week, according to Craig Bandoroff, owner of Denali Stud. Handwalking is essential to a horse's training. The electronic walker builds muscle and fitness, but handwalking teaches the young horses to relax and be better behaved while being led by a handler.

"Sales are our race day, and we have to be ready for it," Bandoroff said. "You want their weight right and muscle right. Once they get into the sale prep program, it is pretty intensive."

Sale preparation begins much earlier for young horses with crooked legs. These horses will often undergo one of two surgical procedures at ten months to straighten their front legs, which may be angled too far outward or inward at the knees.

"They are done starting in January, though some are done as late as May," said Bandoroff. "We like to get them in the winter so we can get the correction we need."

What causes a young horse to develop crooked legs, known as angular limb deformity, is complex, but it is generally accepted that the growth plate on the ends of the long bones above the knee is growing faster on one side. Some horses will straighten on their own with stall rest, careful control of diet, and corrective hoof trimming. Sale horses often undergo surgery, however, because it may take too

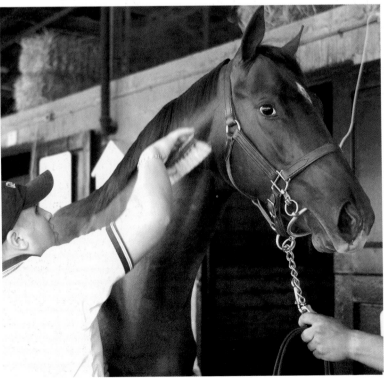

ANNE M. EBERHARDT

It's important for yearlings to look their best on sale day.

long for the problem to correct itself. The crooked legs then become a big liability for the owner.

"The fact of the matter is that you cannot sell a crooked one," Bandoroff said. "We are in the business to maximize our investments."

Horses that undergo surgery will have a portion of the periosteum (the fibrous sheath that covers the bone) cut and lifted away from the bone on the side of the growth plate where development is slower. The incision is made to stimulate bone growth. On the other side of the growth plate, a surgeon will slow or stop the growth by anchoring screws into the bones above and below the growth plate then wrap steel wire between the screws. The second procedure uses a steel staple instead of screws and wires. A staple is hammered into the growth plate on the same side that the screws and wires would be used.

Corrective surgery is controversial because some buyers think the sellers are hiding flaws that should be disclosed, particularly if the horses they buy go on to become breeding stock.

"I can see the negative side from a buyer's point of view about masking the true genetic component of a horse, but I take the approach that the horse will be a sounder, more productive racehorse," Bandoroff said. "I don't think there is anything unethical about it. If someone comes to the barn and asks if the procedure was done, I'll tell them because I don't think it is a big deal."

What would be a big deal, Bandoroff said, is if disclosure becomes mandatory and consignors become responsible for ver-

> ## THINGS TO KNOW
>
> Yearling sales preparation includes exercise in the electric walker.
>
> Some yearlings undergo corrective surgery to straighten crooked legs. Corrective surgery is controversial but some horsemen think it creates a sounder horse.

ifying whether a horse they are selling has had corrective surgery.

"What holds everything up is the record keeping," Bandoroff said. "If I sell a yearling for someone and they don't tell me [surgery] was done, then how can I be responsible? Who is responsible for making sure the medical record follows the horse? Once the industry gets the record keeping in place, then we can start talking [about mandatory disclosure]."

Ciaran Dunne, a yearling-to-juvenile pinhooker and owner of Wavertree Farm near Ocala, Florida, said it doesn't bother him if a yearling has had its legs corrected surgically.

ANNE M. EBERHARDT

Craig Bandoroff of Denali Stud.

ANNE M. EBERHARDT

Straight legs are thought to improve soundness.

"Anything that gets a horse's legs sitting better underneath it will only help," Dunne said, adding that he does not think mandatory disclosure is required.

Maurice W. Miller III, a yearling-to-juvenile pinhooker who operates out of Windhaven Farm near Versailles, Kentucky, also said corrective surgery doesn't concern him.

"As far as the soundness of the horse, it is a good procedure," Miller said. "The only negative is

down the road for the breed. The owner may not know the traits that could be passed along by a horse as a stallion or mare. It's all good as long as it is disclosed."

Juvenile Pinhooks

Surgeries are rare among yearling-to-juvenile pinhooks. With these horses, education and conditioning are everything. Not only do these horses have to look like top-notch sale horses, but they also have to be ready for life at the track.

Dunne, a native of Kildare, Ireland, oversees the breaking of about eighty yearlings a year. In 2005, forty-six of the sixty-two juveniles offered at auction by Dunne's Wavertree Stable were pinhooks. Thirty of the pinhooked horses were sold for a total of $3,122,400 and an average of $242,117, which made Wavertree the fifth-leading juvenile consign-

---

THINGSTO**KNOW**

Yearlings usually begin the breaking process in September.

Walking in the shed row then work in the round pen follow initial breaking.

After about eight weeks sales prospects go to the training track.

---

or by average price in North America. While almost all of the horses he'll handle are owned by a partnership, Dunne said he tries to keep a piece of every one.

The yearlings he and his team of buyers select are shipped directly to Wavertree Farm. Some buyers, particularly those who live out of state, will ship their newly bought horses to a boarding farm near the sales grounds while they make more permanent arrangements. The sale horses will lay over for a few days or a week before being shipped to a training center. Dunne said the sales are stressful enough and he avoids laying over at a farm unless a horse shows signs of getting sick.

As at most other training centers, Wavertree begins breaking in September. The horses are divided into groups of ten, and a new group is started every five days. The first week, horses are kept in their stalls, where they are led in circles and taught to stop on voice command. During the second week of training, a surcingle is added to the turning and voice commands. A surcingle is typically a fleece-lined leather strap that encircles the horse's girth. By using it first, the horse gets accustomed to the pressure of the girth before it's fitted with a saddle. By week three a horse will feel a saddle and the weight of a rider on its back.

"We'll have different riders getting on every horse during this time," Dunne said. "If you have a horse that is acting a little funny, we may keep one rider with him for a while, but we don't want any horse broke to one person. Riders get horses into habits, whether they are right-handed or left-handed or stronger on one leg or another. Hopefully, they don't pick up any bad habits from any one rider."

LOUISE E. REINAGEL

Early lessons on the training track.

During weeks four and five, grooms will walk the horses with riders up in a shed row. The horses will be jogging five to ten minutes by the end of this period and practicing circles in the corners of the shed row. Dunne said the horse is learning to obey the rider during this phase.

Round-pen work begins during the sixth week and lasts for about ten days. In the round pen, the horses will jog in both directions and continue learning how to turn in response to commands from the rider. The horses also are learning to keep their attention on the rider in gradually more open spaces. At the end of each day, the horses at this stage are lined up next to each other so they get used to having other horses close at their sides.

"One horse is always confident. Nothing bothers him," Dunne said. "If you can teach the timid ones to stand beside these more confident horses, they get used to following them and build their own confidence. If a horse is struggling at any point to keep up, we'll drop him back to a later group."

By the seventh week, the horses are jogging in figure-eights in a one-acre paddock and learning to switch leads. Dunne said he starts cantering the horses in a paddock because they naturally switch leads in that tight of an area. If the riders are doing their job, they will be cueing the horses every time the leads should switch. Also during this time, horses in each training group will be divided into two lines. With horses side by side, the lines will face one another. The spacing between the horses is wide enough for another horse to pass between them. The lines of horses then walk toward and between one another like performers in a marching band. The horses will turn around to face each other and

Horses of comparable ability work together.

LOUISE E. REINAGEL

make several more passes. Dunne said a horse must become accustomed to having horses come at him and resist the urge to follow. Later in their racing careers, young horses will see horses jogging toward them during morning workouts at the racetrack. Horses galloping or jogging at the racetrack travel in the opposite direction of the horses that are breezing.

The young racing prospects are ready for the training track after about eight weeks. Each day they go to the track, the horses will pass through a starting gate on the way in and pass through it again on the way back to the barn.

"We do as much gate work as early as we can before they get too fit," Dunne said. "Once they are fit, they get flighty." The horses will go into the gate then jog out in pairs. When they are fit enough to breeze, they are ready to do serious gate work.

"Everything we do is geared toward not getting into a fight with the rider," Dunne said. "We have to let them see that it is their idea, and it is fun."

In late December, the horses will be allowed to run for an eighth of a mile or fifteen seconds at the end of their gallops. Horses of comparable abilities work together. Dunne said it is important that a horse feel challenged without being overmatched. Once a horse can breeze a quarter-mile in thirty seconds, he is ready for some serious work, according to Dunne.

"The hardest thing to learn with pinhooking is that you can't put a round peg into a square hole," he said. "We have horses doing it because they want to do it. We make them make us move them to the next level. We don't increase

speed or distance until they show us they need to do more."

Another challenge with pinhooking juveniles is figuring out where to sell them. Consignors have to make this decision in October, about a month and a half before a horse has shown what it can really do at the track.

"We try to sort them out early, who looks like the physically and mentally forward horses," Dunne said. "We don't train them any earlier; they just move up more quickly.

"Everyone in our business will be loath to say anything [about a horse's ability] in October. Speed work is the making or breaking of a racehorse. When the good ones get to do it, it is like reward. The light goes on, and they really enjoy it. The bad ones hate it."

The Value of Speed

Juvenile sale prospects get to show off their speed during under-tack shows, of which there are two held the week before a sale. While consignors of juveniles approach the under-tack shows with a variety of strategies, the goal is the same — make the horse work in the best time that it is capable of running. Most horses will only breeze a furlong (equal to one-eighth of a mile) and only during the first under-tack show. All 251

THINGS TO KNOW

Sales companies hold two under-tack shows at which juvenile prospects can show their speed.

Shaving off a fifth of a second can increase the price of a juvenile by up to $43,000, according to a study.

Demanding speed in juveniles is a controversial subject.

horses entered in the 2006 Fasig-Tipton select two-year-olds sale at Calder Race Course appeared on Calder's main track during the first under-tack show February 19. Of these, 209 (83 percent) breezed one-eighth of a mile and 36 (14 percent) worked a quarter mile.

Dunne said he thinks the first under-tack show is the more important.

"No one wants to hear any excuses about why one doesn't work," he said. "A horse can move himself up during the second breeze, but that's rare."

The second breeze used to be the more important, but that changed about five years ago when the sales companies began taping the first under-tack works. Many trainers now don't want to devote two weeks to a juvenile sale, coming a week early to watch the works and then staying for the auction. Many will arrive at a sale later and make their short lists of horses to consider based on the videos of the first works. When the Fasig-Tipton Calder sale held its second under-tack show on February 26, 2006, only 159 of the horses worked. Of those, 152 horses had worked during the first under-tack show and thirteen were able to shave off a few tenths of a second from the time of their first work and capture the co-highest work of the day — an eighth of a mile in :10 1/5.

Some consignors will push their horses to work a quarter mile because they believe it creates a better impression in the minds of trainers. Thirty-five horses that had worked an eighth of a mile during the first Fasig-Tipton Calder under-tack show went on to work a quarter mile during the second show.

Juveniles breeze for prospective buyers during under-tack shows.

ANNE M. EBERHARDT

Buyers put a premium on speed.

Dunne said he thinks an eighth of a mile is adequate for horses so young.

"To work them an eighth, a horse has to break about a sixteenth before the eighth-mile pole so he is going full tilt when the timer starts," he said. "Then you have to gallop them out another eighth. If you were to work them a quarter, then you're galloping out another quarter or even three-eighths. It's asking a lot."

Horsemen lament that juveniles are pushed to work in ten seconds or less for an eighth of a mile, but buyers put a premium on speed. In a 2004 study comparing under-tack times and prices, *The Blood-Horse MarketWatch* shows a direct correlation between faster times and higher prices. How much is a fifth of a second worth? About $43,000. When they sold at juve-nile auctions between 2000 and 2002, horses that had worked an eighth of a mile in :10 2/5 brought an average of $171,846 compared with horses that had worked in :10 3/5, which brought an average of $128,958. The study also notes that forty-eight stakes winners and twenty-one graded stakes winners were among the horses that worked a quarter mile between :21 4/5 and :22 2/5, which is almost pedestrian by today's standards.

Preparing To Sell

The weeks leading up to a sale inundate consignors with a deluge of details. One of the most important is getting a set of radiographs taken of every horse's legs, and an endoscope exam video of each horse's throat so that veterinarians can assess the potential for breath-

59

ing problems. A total of thirty-two radiographs (eight pictures at different angles of each leg) are taken within two weeks of the sale for the yearlings. The cost is $600 for digitals and $550 for film. Each endoscope exam costs about $150. For two-year-olds, the radiographs are taken after the first under-tack show. Many juvenile consignors will also supply endoscope videos. This information is then stored in the sale company's repository. This service was introduced at the 1996 Keeneland July select yearling sale as a way to save buyers money, free up time for consignors, and minimize the wear and tear on sale horses that were being subject to multiple pre-sale endoscope exams. Putting radiographs in the repository has become essential for yearling sales, but endoscopic exam videos are hardly ever taken. "Buyers want to do it themselves and make their own evaluation because it is a fluid situation," Bandoroff said. "A horse could be fine one day and not the next." A popular horse may get scoped ten to fifteen times before it sells, while a horse getting moderate attention may get scoped up to four times, according to Bandoroff.

Despite the conveniences it does offer, the repository is still not an entirely welcome addition.

"The only thing buyers use a repository for is to eliminate horses," Dunne said. He added that any serious buyer is going to take another set of radiographs anyway.

"It is amazing how much you can learn to live with after you've bought them, than before you buy them," Dunne said. "The ones that have to go back, go back. If you find a chip, the owner might decide to

have the surgery and go on."

The potential for rumors to spread in a repository is also a concern. If three or four people are in the repository looking at radiographs, and one person makes a comment like, "Boy, I sure don't like that dark spot there." The comment may be overheard and shared outside the repository.

"If the word gets out that a horse didn't vet clean, whether it is legitimate or not, it hurts the horse," Dunne said. "If we didn't have [the repository], we might sell horses for a little less, but we might sell more of them."

Bandoroff said he doesn't mind having the repository.

"I think it has facilitated the ability to sell horses," he said. "I don't worry about rumors because I like to think these people are professionals and are capable of making their own decisions." The cost is the main drawback Bandoroff sees with repositories.

"It concerns me that the cost is totally born by the seller and not shared by the consumer," he said.

Costs

Pinhooking is an attractive way to participate in the horse industry because the horse is only owned for a limited amount of time, which reduces the expenses and risks otherwise assumed by breeders and racehorse owners. The venture is still not cheap, however.

The general estimated cost of getting a weanling to a yearling sale is $10,000. If the horse needs corrective surgery, that will cost another $2,000 approximately. Costs vary considerably from region to region in the United States. An informal cost survey in 2004 of *The Blood-Horse MarketWatch* subscribers shows that the average monthly bill for weanlings ranged from $823 per month in Kentucky to $504 per month in the Southwest. Additional expenses arrive with the sale. The consignor has to bring grooms to care for the horses and, for the bigger outfits, hire additional people to show the horses to prospective buyers. A nice sale halter also needs to be purchased along with a stall card, which is like an advertisement posted on the wall outside a sale horse's stall. In all, these additional expenses could reach $1,000. All these costs do not include the consignor's commission, which is usually about 5 percent if the horse sells and about 3.5 percent of the fall-of-the-hammer price if the horse is bought back.

For yearling-to-juvenile pinhooks, the cost of breaking and getting a horse to a sale is $20,000-$25,000 at the most. This estimate, as with the yearlings, does not include the costs incurred during a sale or the consignor's commission. Several juvenile pinhooks are owned by partnerships, and the managers of these partnerships assess the owners in a number of different ways. Investors need to know up front how these expenses will be billed because costs can escalate quickly. For example, a consignor may aim a two-year-old in training for the Fasig-Tipton Calder sale. The horse gets shipped to the track in Opa-locka north of Miami, goes through the under-tack shows, and then becomes sick or injured. Now you have the unwelcome expense of shipping the horse back to the farm or training center then paying all the costs of sending him to another sale

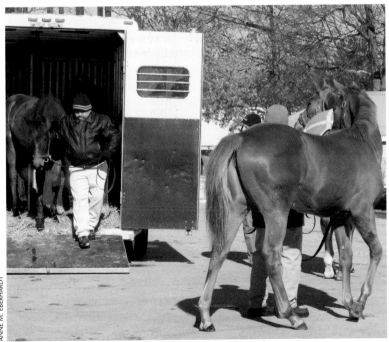

ANNE M. EBERHARDT

Among the costs associated with pinhooking is shipping to the sales.

later in the year.

Some partnerships try to minimize this potential aggravation for investors by estimating up front the total cost of getting a horse broken, trained, and to the next sale and then pro-rate the expenses monthly. The sooner a horse sells, the less the owner pays. One company eliminates the monthly bills by syndicating its entire crop of yearling-to-juvenile pinhooks. First, the company estimates how much cash it will need to support a syndicate of seventeen to eighteen horses. The $25,000 per head cost of breaking, training, regular veterinary care, etc., is included with an estimated cost of buying the horses. An investor then buys a share in the group of horses to be pinhooked for a fixed cost, for example, $100,000, and will never see another invoice. If the syndicate managers get the cost estimate wrong, they have to eat it.

Odds and Ends

Public auctions generate a lot of paperwork. Denali Stud has a full-time employee who does nothing but keep track of all the forms that must be submitted. There are sales nomination forms, nominations to a variety of state-bred incentive programs, health certificates, and a negative Coggins test (meaning the horse has not been exposed to equine infectious anemia) required for each sale prospect. Consignors and partnerships are more than willing to take care of the paperwork so they can be sure everything gets done. Owners also should expect to sign a form that authorizes a consignor to act as their agent during the auction and a sales contract that spells out any additional charges that may be incurred plus the commission to be paid.

What an owner sees when he arrives at the sale is the summit of a rather tall mountain. The consignment is working like clockwork, shuttling horses in and out of their stalls to be inspected by buyers. These horses are in top condition, sculpted by months of careful preparation. All the work has been done with the sole purpose of making a horse's two-minute appearance on an auction stage the best it can be. Hopefully, those pinhookers who have carefully prepared for this moment will reap the rewards and be able to end the day with a celebration.

— *Eric Mitchell*

7

Pinhooking "Home Runs"

Pinhooking is hard work. You've got to search through thousands of horses to find just a handful you like that you also can buy for reasonable prices. Then you've got to hope nothing goes wrong before you resell them.

The potential pitfalls are numerous. Horses get injured, or they don't work fast. They fail to develop physically, turning from beautiful swans into ugly ducklings in just a few months.

So why do pinhookers keep coming back year after year, making a career out of one of the Thoroughbred industry's riskiest ventures? It's the prospect of a huge financial windfall.

At the time this book was published, the biggest pot of gold at the end of the pinhooking rainbow involved a son of Forestry named The Green Monkey. Florida horse-men Randy Hartley and Dean De Renzo purchased the colt for $425,000 at the 2005 Fasig-Tipton Kentucky July select yearling sale and then resold him for a world-record auction price of $16 million at the 2006 Fasig-Tipton Florida select sale of two-year-olds in training at Calder Race Course. In less than a year, The Green Monkey increased in value by an astound-

The Green Monkey in action before the sale.

LOUISE E. REINAGEL

Randy Hartley and Dean De Renzo, who consigned The Green Monkey.

ing $15,575,000.

Hartley and De Renzo have years of experience in the pinhooking game, and their knowledge, no doubt, played a role in their success. But it also took a lot of luck.

Hartley had decided to drop out of the bidding for The Green Monkey when the colt was a yearling because he thought the price had gotten too high. But De Renzo jumped back in at the last minute, a move Hartley didn't agree with at the time.

"The whole way home, Dean was asking me, 'Did we give too much?' and I didn't want to say, 'Heck yeah,' even though I was thinking it," Hartley said. "I just told him, 'No, it will be all right.' "

To their credit, the colt had an attractive pedigree. His second dam, Nannerl, was a grade II winner and the dam of a grade II-winning daughter of Storm Cat, Magicalmysterycat. He also was impressive physically, with a lot of bone and a long body.

But everything had to go just

right for Hartley and De Renzo to reap their gigantic reward. First, the colt turned in the fastest work at an eighth of a mile in a preview show before the Fasig-Tipton Florida sale, covering the distance in :09 4/5. He also did it in a relaxed, easy manner.

Then, he caught the eyes of two of the most powerful auction buyers, Sheikh Mohammed of Dubai and Irish agent Demi O'Byrne of the Coolmore Stud team.

After less than four minutes of bidding, The Green Monkey's price passed $5.2 million, the previous world-record auction amount for a two-year-old in training. After less than eight minutes, it soared by the $13.1-million world mark for any Thoroughbred ever offered at public auction.

O'Byrne was the winner, making Hartley and De Renzo the richest pinhookers after a one-horse transaction.

The previous pinhooking record paled in comparison. It was owned by Robert V. LaPenta and a son of

Fusaichi Pegasus named Fusaichi Samurai. LaPenta had purchased Fusaichi Samurai for $270,000 at the 2003 Fasig-Tipton Saratoga select yearling sale. In 2004, through Kip Elser's Kirkwood Stables, LaPenta resold the colt for $4.5 million at the Fasig-Tipton Florida auction to Fusao Sekiguchi. Fusaichi Samurai's juvenile price represented an appreciation in value of $4,230,000.

Dubai Dream, a son of Stephen Got Even, enjoyed an appreciation in value of $2,943,000 when he brought $3.1 million at the 2004 Fasig-Tipton Florida auction. His yearling purchase price was $157,000.

Before then, the biggest appreciation in value for a two-year-old sold at public auction was $2,670,000. Diamond Fury, a son

of Sea of Secrets, was a $30,000 yearling in 2002 and then brought $2.7 million at the 2003 Barretts March select sale of two-year-olds in training.

In 2006 alone, no fewer than nineteen pinhooked juveniles sold at public auction appreciated in value by $500,000 or more from their previous purchase prices. Five appreciated in value by $1 million or more. In 2005, fourteen appreciated in value by $500,000 or more.

Weanling-to-yearling pinhook-

LESLIE MARTIN

Fusaichi Samurai, a $4.5 million juvenile, sold for $270,000 as a yearling.

LESLIE MARTIN

Dubai Dream fetched $3.1 million in 2004. He cost $157,000 as a yearling.

ers haven't enjoyed scores that are as lucrative at the top end of their market, but they have collected some impressive profits.

The North American auction record, as of this book's publication, is the $1,180,000 appreciation in value by Dubai Touch. B.M.K. Equine bought the son of Saint Ballado as a weanling for $220,000 at the 1999 Keeneland November breeding stock sale. The following year, Hartwell Farm, agent, resold Dubai Touch for $1.4 million to John Ferguson Bloodstock at the Keeneland July select yearling sale.

The former mark for appreciation in value of $1,015,000 belonged to Talk Is Money, a son of Deputy Minister. He sold for $1.8 million during the 1999 Keeneland September yearling auction after bringing $785,000 as a weanling in November at Keeneland the previous year.

Since 2000, two yearlings have appreciated in value by $1 million or more from their weanling sale price. They are Seeking an Alibi, a son of Storm Cat, and Lifestyle, a son of Indian Charlie.

Kentucky bloodstock agent Peter Bradley headed a partnership that purchased Seeking an Alibi for $500,000 at the 2002 Keeneland November sale. When the colt was resold through Eaton Sales, agent, at the 2003 Keeneland September yearling sale, he brought a $1.6-million winning bid from John

Ferguson, representing Sheikh Mohammed of Dubai. Seeking an Alibi's appreciation in value was $1.1 million.

Paul Paternostro and James Herbener, in the name of Holiday Stables, bought Lifestyle as a weanling for $100,000 at Keeneland in November of 2000. They resold the colt for $1.1 million to Prince Ahmed Salman's The Thoroughbred Corp. at the 2001 Keeneland September yearling auction.

In 2005, four pinhooked yearlings were resold for prices that increased their value by $500,000 or more apiece from their weanling purchase prices. The number was three in 2004.

The Blood-Horse does not keep records of financial windfalls that pinhookers have enjoyed for mares. But a quick review of the mares sold during the 2006 Keeneland January horses of all ages sale shows that this can be a lucrative venture when mares are claimed on the racetrack for modest prices.

Trainer Michael Stidham claimed Dance Tune, a daughter of French Deputy, for $25,000 in October 2005 at Keeneland. Dance Tune had three career victories and a third-place finish in the 2005 Carousel Stakes at Oaklawn Park. Her family members included Canadian champion Term Limits. Consigned by James Keogh, agent, to the 2006 Keeneland January sale, Dance Tune sold to Stonewall Farm & Atoka for $270,000.

Glory of Love, a daughter of Not For Love, also experienced a big jump in value. A seven-time winner, she finished second in the 2005 Conniver Stakes at Laurel Park and third in the 2004 Alma North Stakes at Timonium. Trainer Scott Lake claimed her for $50,000 on behalf of Home Team Stables at

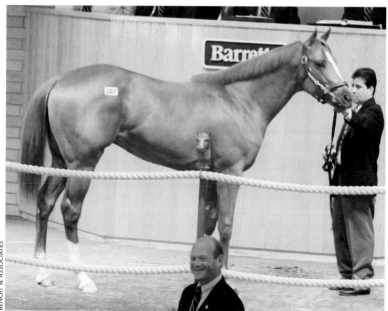

BENOIT & ASSOCIATES

Diamond Fury, a $2.7 million Barretts graduate.

Delaware Park in August 2005. Also consigned by Keogh, as agent, to the 2006 Keeneland January sale, she sold for $195,000 to Stonewall Farm & Atoka.

But while there's potential for big financial scores in the pinhooking game, there's also the possibility of a financial wipeout. The examples are numerous and can be found in virtually every auction where pinhooked horses are sold. Here are just a few from the 2006 juvenile selling season:

• Ticket Home, a son of Grand Slam, was sold for only $40,000 at the Fasig-Tipton Florida auction after being purchased as a yearling for $310,000.

• Prime Ruler, a son of Orientate, was sold for $200,000 at the Barretts May sale after being purchased as a yearling for $400,000.

• A Storm Cat—Blissful colt was sold for $90,000 at the Fasig-Tipton Florida auction after being purchased as a yearling for $180,000. *— Deirdre B. Biles*

Frequently Asked Questions

How do I choose the right horse for a pinhooking venture?

You need to start with a search for the right people to assist you. Because of the risks associated with pinhooking, a team of advisors is considered crucial. Depending on the type of venture, professional advisers should include bankers, lawyers, accountants, insurance agents, bloodstock agents, trainers, and veterinarians.

You also need to decide whether you want to buy a horse to pinhook as a yearling, a two-year-old, or broodmare prospect. Each category has its advantages and disadvantages. Note that the purchase of yearlings to resell as two-year-olds represents the majority of pinhooking efforts.

The price level at which you feel comfortable risking is important considerations. It's important to be current on trends in the marketplace, such as which sires are popular, represent value, or might be overlooked.

How do I decide which type of pinhooking is best for me?

Explore each segment of the pinhooking market and see which fits into your game plan and finances. Buying a weanling to sell as

a yearling is less costly and less risky but usually reaps fewer financial windfalls. Investing in a yearling to sell as a two-year-old requires a larger investment because the youngster will have to be sent to a farm for breaking and training. The juvenile also will be breezed for potential buyers at the two-year-old sale, a rite of passage that could make or break you. Pinhooking broodmares requires time and energy if you plan to manage the endeavor. It also requires a larger investment — the stud fee, transportation to and from the stallion, veterinary bills all add to the cost.

You may also want to consider pinhooking partnerships. Like racing partnerships, these investment groups allow you to participate

ANNE M. EBERHARDT

Have a game plan before you get started.

while reducing your cost and spreading out the risk. There are a wide variety of partnerships available so be sure you understand all the details up front.

Which segment of the pinhooking market is the most profitable?

Buying yearlings to sell as two-year-olds is usually the most lucrative prospect. Pinhookers historically have done well in this segment of the market, which produces Thoroughbreds that are of or nearing racing age. It's the largest segment of the market, with plenty of competition. But, if you have a well-conformed prospect that breezes quickly and has a decent pedigree, there will be plenty of people willing to get in on the bidding.

What are the chances of making a profit?

Depending on whom you talk to, one-quarter to one-half of all pinhooking prospects make a profit. Pinhookers hit "home runs" every year, and it is not uncommon for pinhookers to double

their investment. Nevertheless, pinhookers should be prepared to lose their investment, and more, if their pinhook prospects fail to develop or elicit interest from buyers.

What are the risks associated with pinhooking?

Pinhooking is fraught with risks. A weanling bought for resale as a yearling might fail to outgrow conformation faults and prove unattractive to buyers. A yearling bought for resale as a two-year-old might not show speed in the all-important under-tack shows. A filly purchased as a broodmare prospect might have reproductive problems that prevent her from getting in foal. In addition, horses of any age are subject to injury or illness that might preclude their resale.

What are the costs associated with bringing a pinhook prospect to market?

In addition to the purchase price, costs include boarding, insurance, conditioning, training (for two-year-old prospects), veteri-

Bringing a horse to market is the ultimate test of pinhooking skill.

nary and farrier care, and transportation. The general estimated cost of getting a weanling to a yearling sale is $10,000. If the horse needs corrective surgery, that will cost another $2,000 approximately. For yearling-to-juvenile pinhooks, the cost of breaking and getting a horse to a sale is $20,000-$25,000 at the most.

What if my horse does not sell?

This is a question you need answered before you start. The bloodstock agent/consignor must be able to give you all the options, particularly if you are not interested in racing. Typically, a horse that does not meet its reserve price can be sold privately back in the barn. You need an agent who is keeping tabs on the buyers interested in your horse and can put this kind of deal together.

If you are involved in a weanling-to-yearling pinhook, you may be able to offer your horse through another sale. You may also want to consider holding on to it and reselling it as a two-year-old. Going to another sale means more shipping and sales-related expenses. Waiting to sell a horse as a two-year-old means the additional cost of breaking and training, six to seven months of care, and lots of additional risk. Weigh your options carefully. Often, it is better to sell a horse privately at a loss than assume the additional expense and risk.

What types of veterinary exams should a pinhooking prospect undergo?

Weanlings, yearlings, and two-year-olds should undergo endoscopic exams of the airways to rule

ANNE M. EBERHARDT

Scoping is an important pre-sale test.

out any restrictions or breathing problems. Radiographs should be taken of the front and hind fetlocks as well as knees, stifles, and hocks. Most sales companies have a repository where veterinary records can be reviewed by the buyer's veterinarian. In addition to being inspected for physical conformation, broodmares should undergo a reproductive exam to ensure they are capable of becoming pregnant and maintaining pregnancy.

What are the most important considerations in buying a pinhooking prospect?

Ideally, buyers want as much pedigree as possible in an excellent physical specimen. Good conformation is crucial, especially clean, straight legs. At the same time, experts note that young horses can change significantly, especially weanlings, so some conformation flaws might be forgiven.

Resale value also is extremely important, so a horse has to have an attractive enough pedigree to interest buyers. A strategy pinhookers use to cut costs is to buy the offspring of first-crop stallions, which have no proven runners. Consequently, their offspring might be less expensive. That approach, however, has become popular in recent years, making fewer bargains available.

Experts also consider the pedigree and the produce record of the horse's dam. They will take a chance on a first foal of a particular mare as she has no blemish yet on her produce record.

Should all business agreements and other contracts be in writing?

Some kinds of contracts, including documents relating to the sale of real property, must be in writing. Generally, though, a court will enforce an oral contract if the existence of the agreement and its terms can be proved. One advantage of using written contracts is that the practice encourages the parties to put more thought into the agreement, which may make disputes less likely. A good rule of thumb is that an agreement should be in writing unless you are willing to accept the consequences of a breach of the contract by the other party.

How can I locate an attorney or accountant with expertise in equine law?

The best source of information is a referral from a friend or acquaintance in the horse business who has utilized the professional's services in the past. This shouldn't be a problem in locations with large equine populations. Some state or local bar associations offer a lawyer referral service that evaluates the needs of a client and then attempts to match that person with an attorney knowledgeable in the field. Many lawyer referral services have minimum educational or experience requirements for an attorney to be listed in a particular area of expertise. Advertising on the Internet or in other sources may be the least reliable way to identify a competent professional. Whatever route leads you to the office of a particular attorney or accountant, you should ask enough questions at the first meeting to satisfy yourself that the professional has the skills and the time to represent your interests adequately.

Conformation

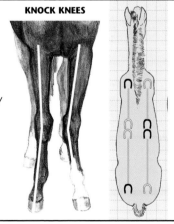

	NORMAL END FRONT	**BASE NARROW**
Joint Problem/ Typical Flight Pattern		
Probable Stresses	No abnormal stresses	(Front): Compression of the lateral side of the knee, fetlock, and hoof (Hind): Compression of the lateral side of the hock, fetlock, and hoof
Gait Problem/ Common Injuries	None	Landing on the lateral side (outside) of the hoof, lateral ringbone, lateral wind puffs, lateral sidebone, lateral heel bruising
	KNOCK KNEES	**BOW LEGS**
Joint Problem/ Typical Flight Pattern		
Probable Stresses	Tension on the medial collateral ligaments of the knee, compression of the lateral surface of the knee, stress on joints proximal to the knee	Tension on the lateral collateral ligaments of the knee, compression of the medial surface of the knee, stress on joints proximal to the knee
Gait Problem/ Common Injuries	Varying degrees of outward rotation of the cannon bone, fetlock, and foot usually accompany this problem. Flight and landing vary depending on other problems.	Often accompanied by base narrow, toed in conformation. Flight and landing vary depending on other problems.

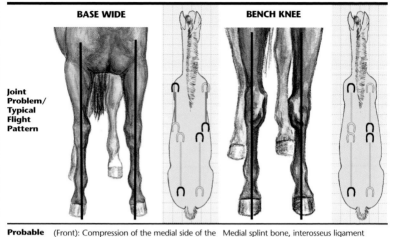

	BASE WIDE	**BENCH KNEE**
Joint Problem/ Typical Flight Pattern		
Probable Stresses	(Front): Compression of the medial side of the knee, fetlock, and hoof (Hind): Compression of the medial side of the hock, fetlock, and hoof	Medial splint bone, interosseus ligament
Gait Problems/ Common Injuries	Landing on the medial side (inside) of the hoof, medial ringbone, medial sidebone, medial wind puffs, medial heel bruising	Medial splints. Flight and landing vary depending on other problems.

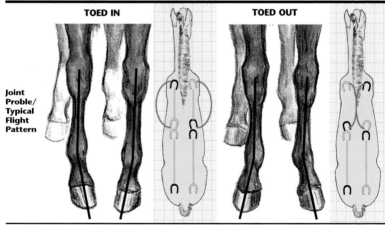

	TOED IN	**TOED OUT**
Joint Proble/ Typical Flight Pattern		
Probable Stresses	Stress associated with breaking over the out-side (lateral side) of the toe	Stress associated with breaking over the inside (medial) side of the toe
Gait Problem/ Common Injuries	Paddling foot flight; landing on lateral hoof edge; lateral ringbone, wind puffs, sidebone, heel bruising. Can involve angle of legs from body, knee/hock, and/or fetlock.	Winging in flight, can hit other leg; landing on medial hoof edge; medial ringbone, sidebone, wind puffs, heel bruising. Can involve leg angle from body, knee/hock, and/or fetlock.

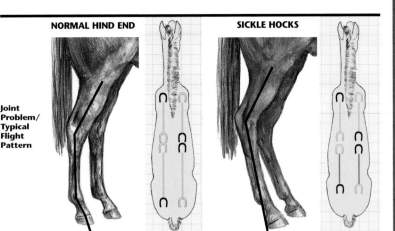

	NORMAL HIND END	**SICKLE HOCKS**
Joint Problem/ Typical Flight Pattern		
Probable Stresses	No abnormal stresses	Plantar ligaments ("behind" the leg)
Gait Problem/ Common Injuries	None	Curb (enlargement of the rearward aspect of the fibular tarsal bone due to inflammation and thickening of the plantar ligament).

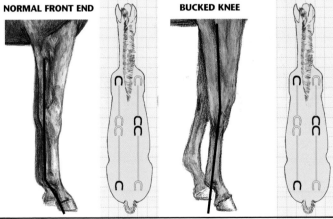

	NORMAL FRONT END	**BUCKED KNEE**
Joint Problem/ Typical Flight Pattern		
Probable Stresses	No abnormal stresses	Sesamoid bones, superficial flexor tendon, extensor carpi radialis, suspensory ligament
Gait Problem/ Common Injuries	None	Usually cased by contraction of the carpal flexors. Flight and landing vary depending on other problems.

	STRAIGHT HOCKS	**BOW HOCKS**
Joint Problem/ Typical Flight Pattern	 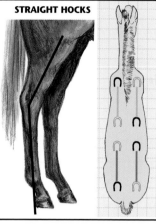	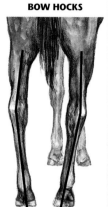 
Probable Stresses	Tension on the dorsal aspect of the joint capsule, irritation and chronic distension of the joint capsule	Excessive strain on the lateral side of the hock joint
Gait Problems/ Common Injuries	Bog spavin (chronic distension of tibiotarsal joint capsule of hock, causing swelling of dorsomedial aspect of hock), upward fixation of the patella. Pasterns are often straight.	Horses with bow hocks are often toed in and base narrow behind. Flight and landing vary depending on other problems.

	CALF KNEE	**LONG, WEAK PASTERN**
Joint Problem/ Typical Flight Pattern	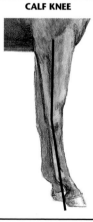	  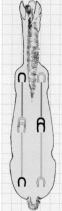
Probable Stresses	Carpal/radial check ligaments, proximal middle/distal accessory carpal ligaments, palmar carpal ligament, compression of front of the knee	Suspensory apparatus, flexor tendons
Gait Problems/ Common Injuries	Chip fractures of third, radial, and intermediate carpal bones and radius. Knee tends to flex backward especially in tired horse. Flight/landing vary depending on other problems.	Tenosynovitis, suspensory ligament desmitis

COW HOCKS

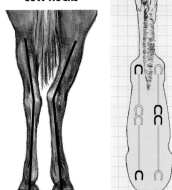

Joint Problem/ Typical Flight Pattern

Probable Stresses
Excessive strain on the medial side of the hock joint

Gait Problems/ Common Injuries
Bone spavin. Horses with cow hocks are often sickle-hocked and toed out as well. Flight and landing vary depending on other problems.

SHORT, UPRIGHT PASTERN

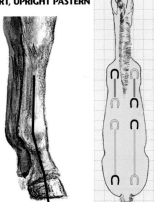

Joint Proble/ Typical Flight Pattern

Probable Stresses
Increased concussion on the fetlock joint, pastern joint, and navicular bone

Gait Problems/ Common Injuries
Osselets (traumatic arthritis of the fetlock), ringbone of the pastern joint. Often accompanied by an upright shoulder.

Illustrations courtesy of Robin Peterson

Resource Guide

This listing includes the types of sales offered, the month the sale is generally held, and the location. To find out specific sales dates, contact the sales company for a complete schedule and to receive catalogs.

American Equine Sales
4061 E. Castro Valley Blvd.
Suite 276
Castro Valley, CA 94552
(510) 293-9330
www.americanequinesales.com
> *Two-year-olds in training*
>> *June — Alameda County Fairgrounds, Pleasanton, Calif.*
> *Yearlings*
>> *August — Alameda County Fairgrounds*

Arizona Thoroughbred Breeders Association
P.O. Box 41774, Phoenix, AZ 85050
(602) 942-1310
www.atba.net
> *Mixed*
>> *October — Westworld, Scottsdale, Ariz.*

Arkansas Thoroughbred Sales Co.
P.O. Box 180159
Fort Smith, AR 72918
(501) 648-3402
> *Mixed*
>> *February, October — Barton Coliseum, State Fairgrounds, Little Rock, Ark.*

Barretts Equine Ltd.
P.O. Box 2010, Pomona, CA 91769
(909) 629-3099
www.barretts.com
> *Mixed — January*
> *Two-year-olds in training — March*
> *Two-year-olds in training, horses of racing age — May*
> *Mixed — October*
> *Yearlings — October*
>> *(all held at Fairplex Park, Pomona, Calif.)*

Breeders Sales Company of Louisiana
P.O. Box 24650
New Orleans, LA 70184
(504) 947-4676
www.louisianabred.com
> *Yearlings, mixed*
>> *September — Louisiana Downs, Bossier City, La.*

California Thoroughbred Breeders Association (CTBA)
P.O. Box 60018
Arcadia, CA 91066
(626) 445-7800
www.ctba.com
> *Yearlings*
>> *August — Del Mar Horse Park, Del Mar, Calif.*

Fair Grounds Sales Company
1751 Gentilly Blvd.
New Orleans, LA 70152
(504) 944-5515
www.fgno.com
> *Two-year-olds in training*
>> *March — Fair Grounds Race Course*

Fasig-Tipton Company
2400 Newtown Pike
P.O. Box 13610
Lexington, KY 40583
(859) 255-1555
www.fasigtipton.com
>   *Mixed — February*
>   *Select Yearlings — July*
>   *Yearlings — October*
>   *Mixed — November*

Fasig-Tipton Florida
21001 N.W. 27th Ave.
Miami, FL 33056
(305) 626-3947
>   *Select two-year-olds in training*
>   *February — Calder Race Course*

Fasig-Tipton Midlantic
356 Fair Hill Drive, Suite C
Elkton, MD 21921
(410) 392-5555
>   *Mixed — February, December*
>   *Two-year-olds in training — May*
>   *Two-year-olds in training, horses of*
>   *racing age — July*
>   *Yearlings — late September/early*
>   *October*
>   *(all held at Timonium Fair*
>   *Grounds)*

Fasig-Tipton New York
40 Elmont Road
Elmont, NY 11003
(516) 328-1800
>   *Select, preferred yearlings*
>   *August — Saratoga*
>   *Horses of racing age*
>   *October — Belmont Park*

Fasig-Tipton Texas
1000 Lone Star Parkway
Grand Prairie, TX 75050
(972) 262-0000
>   *Two-year-olds in training — March*
>   *Yearlings — August*
>   *Mixed — December*
>   *(all held at Lone Star Park)*

Finger Lakes Thoroughbred Sales
P.O. Box 301, Shortsville, NY 14548
(716) 289-8524
www.nybreds.com/GVBA/flsale.html
>   *Mixed*
>   *September — Finger Lakes Race*
>   *Track, Farmington, N.Y.*

Heritage Place
2829 S. MacArthur Blvd.
Oklahoma City, OK 73128
(405) 682-4551
www.heritageplace.com
>   *Mixed*
>   *January, June, October*

**Illinois Thoroughbred Breeders
and Owners Foundation**
P.O. Box 336
Caseyville, IL 62232
(618) 344-3427
www.illinoisracingnews.com
>   *Two-year-olds in training,*
>   *horses of racing age*
>   *June — Arlington Park,*
>   *Arlington Heights, Ill.*
>   *Mixed*
>   *Sept./Oct. — Hawthorne*
>   *Racecourse, Cicero, Ill.*

**Indiana Thoroughbred Owners
and Breeders Association**
P.O. Box 3753, Carmel, IN 46082
(800) 450-9895
www.itoba.com
>   *Mixed*
>   *August — Hoosier Park,*
>   *Anderson, Ind.*

**Iowa Breeders and Owners
Association**
1 Prairie Meadows Drive
Altoona, IA 50009
(515) 967-1298
www.iowathoroughbred.com
>   *Mixed*
>   *September — Iowa State*
>   *Fairgrounds*

Keeneland Association
4201 Versailles Road, P.O. Box 1690
Lexington, KY 40588
(859) 254-3412
www.keeneland.com
>Mixed — January
>Two-year-olds in training — April
>Yearlings — September
>Mixed — November

**Louisiana Thoroughbred
Breeders Sales Co.**
P.O. Box 789, Carencro, LA 70520
(337) 896-6152
E-mail: ltbsc1@aol.com
>Mixed
>>April — Blackham Coliseum,
>>Lafayette, La.
>Mixed
>>August — Blackham Coliseum
>Mixed
>>October/November — Delta
>>Downs Racetrack, Vinton, La.

Ocala Breeders' Sales Company
P.O. Box 99
1701 S.W. 60th Ave.
Ocala, FL 34478
(352) 237-2154
www.obssales.com
>Mixed — January, October
>Select year-olds in training —
>>February, at Calder Race Course
>Two-year-olds in training —
>>March, April
>Two-year-olds in training and
>>Horses of racing age — June
>Yearlings — August

**Oregon Thoroughbred Breeders
Association**
P.O. Box 17248, Portland, OR 97217
(503) 285-0658
thoroughbredinfo.com/showcase/otba.htm
>Mixed
>>September — Oakhurst Ranch,
>>Newburg, Ore.

Ruidoso Select Sales Company
P.O. Box 909
Ruidoso Downs, NM 88346
(505) 378-4474
www.zianet.com/rdracing/HorseSale.htm
>Yearling
>>August — Ruidoso Downs
>>Racetrack, Ruidoso Downs, N.M.

Thomas Sales Company
10410 N. Yale Ave., Sperry, OK 74073
(918) 288-7308
E-mail: thomas.sales@worldnet.att.net
>Mixed
>>February, May, August,
>>November — Expo Fairgrounds,
>>Tulsa, Okla.

**Thoroughbred Horsemen's
Association of Texas**
Rte. 5, Box 172, Bryan, TX 77803
(409) 823-1911

**Washington Thoroughbred
Breeders Association**
P.O. Box 1499, Auburn, WA 98071
(253) 288-7878
www.washingtonthoroughbred.com
>Yearlings
>>September — Emerald Downs
>>Race Track, Auburn, Wash.
>Mixed
>>December — Emerald Downs

Canadian Equine Sales Companies

**Canadian Thoroughbred Horse
Society (Ontario Division)**
P.O. Box 172,
Rexdale, Ontario M9W 5L1
(416) 675-3602
www.cthsont.com
>Two-year-olds in training
>>May — Woodbine Sales Pavilion,
>>Rexdale, Ontario
>Mixed
>>Dec. — Woodbine Sales Pavilion

Canadian Thoroughbred Horse Society (British Columbia Division)
17687 56-A Ave.
Surrey, British Columbia V3S 1G4
(604) 574-0145
www.cthsbc.org
   Mixed
      September — British Columbia

Canadian Thoroughbred Horse Society (Alberta Division)
401, 255-17 Ave., SW
Calgary, Alberta T2S 2T8
(403) 229-3609
www.cthsalta.com
   Mixed
      October — Alberta

Fasig-Tipton at Woodbine
Woodbine Sales Pavilion
555 Rexdale Blvd.
Rexdale, Ontario M9W 5L2
   Yearling — September

Foreign Equine Sales Companies

Agence Française de Vente du Pur-Sang
32, avenue Hocquart-de-Turtot
14803 Deauville, France
+33 2 31 81 81 00
www.deauville-sales.com

Doncaster Bloodstock Sales Ltd.
Auction Mart Offices, Hawick
Roxburghshire, England TD9 9NN
+44 (0)1450 372222
www.dbsautions.com

Goffs Bloodstock Sales Ltd.
Kildare Paddocks, Kill
Co. Kildare, Ireland
+353-45-886600
www.goffs.com

William Inglis & Son Ltd.
Newmarket Stables, Sydney
Young Street, Randwick NSW,
Australia 2031
+61 (02) 9399 7999
www.inglis.com.au

Magic Millions Sales Pty Limited
28 Ascot Court, Bundall
P.O. Box 5246
Gold Coast Mail Centre
Queensland, Australia 4217
+61 (07) 5538 8933
www.magicmillions.com.au

New Zealand Bloodstock Ltd.
Karaka Sales Centre
Hingaia Road, Papakura
P.O. Box 97-447
South Auckland Mail Centre
Auckland, New Zealand
+64 9 298 0055
www.nzb.co.nz

Tattersalls Ltd.
Terrace House
Newmarket, Suffolk, England
CB8 9BT
+44 1638 665931
www.tattersalls.com

National Thoroughbred Associations

The Jockey Club
821 Corporate Drive
Lexington, KY 40503-2794
(859) 224-2700
E-mail: comments@jockeyclub.com
www.home.jockeyclub.com

Thoroughbred Owners and Breeders Association
P.O. Box 4367
Lexington, KY 40544-4367
(859) 276-2291
E-mail: info@toba.org
www.TOBA.org

State Associations

**American Association
of Equine Practitioners**
4075 Iron Works Parkway
Lexington, KY 40511
(859) 233-0147
E-mail: aaepoffice@aaep.org
www.aaep.org

**Arizona Thoroughbred
Breeders Association**
P.O. Box 41774,
Phoenix, AZ 85080
(602) 942-1310
E-mail: atba@worldnet.att.net
www.atba.net

**Arkansas Thoroughbred
Breeders Horsemen's
Association**
P.O. Box 21641
Hot Springs, AR 71903-1641
Phone (501) 624-6328
E-mail: deana@atbha.com
www.atbha.com

**California Thoroughbred
Breeders Association**
201 Colorado Place, Arcadia, CA 91007
(800) 573-2822 or (626) 445-7800
E-mail: info@ctba.com
www.ctba.com

**Florida Thoroughbred
Breeders' and Owners'
Association**
801 SW 60th Ave.
Ocala, FL 34474-1827
(352) 629-2160
E-mail: FTBOA@aol.com
www.ftboa.com

**Georgia Thoroughbred Owners
& Breeders Association**
P.O. Box 987
Tyrone, GA 30290
(770) 451-0409
E-mail: gtoba@msn.com
www.gtoba.com

**Illinois Thoroughbred Breeders
& Owners Foundation**
P.O. Box 336
Caseyville, IL 62232-0336
(618) 344-3427
E-mail: itboffp@apci.net
www.illinoisracingnews.com

**Indiana Thoroughbred
Owners & Breeders
Association**
P.O. Box 3753
Carmel, IN 46082-3753
(800) 450-9895
E-mail: itoba@itoba.com
www.itoba.com

**Iowa Thoroughbred
Breeders & Owners**
1 Prairie Meadows Drive
Altoona, IA 50009
(800) 577-1097 or (515) 967-1298
E-mail:
itboa@prairiemeadows.com
www.iowathoroughbred.com

**Kansas Thoroughbred
Association**
215 Monroe Street
Fredonia, KS 66736-1262
(620) 378-4772
E-mail: gejo@twinmounds.com

**Kentucky Thoroughbred
Owners and Breeders Inc.**
4079 Iron Works Parkway
Lexington, KY 40511-8483
(859) 259-1643
E-mail: contact@kta-ktob.com
www.kta-ktob.com

**Louisiana Thoroughbred
Breeders Association**
P.O. Box 24650
New Orleans, LA 70184
(800) 772-1195
or (504) 943-2149
E-mail: ltba@iamerica.net
www.louisianabred.com

**Maryland Horse Breeders
Association**
P.O. Box 427
Timonium, MD 21094-0427
(410) 252-2100
E-mail:
info@marylandthoroughbred.com
www.marylandthoroughbred.com

**Michigan Thoroughbred
Owners & Breeders
Association**
4800 Harvey Street
Muskegon, MI 49444
(231) 798-7721
E-mail: mtoba@iserv.net
www.mtoba.com

**Minnesota Thoroughbred
Association**
1100 Canterbury Road
Shakopee, MN 55379
(952) 496-3770
E-mail: mtassoc@voyager.net
www.mtassoc.com

**Mississippi Thoroughbred
Owners & Breeders Association**
107 Sundown
Madison, MS 39110
(601) 856-8293

**Missouri Horse Racing
Association**
19900 South State Rt. 7
Pleasant Hill, MO 64080
(816) 987-3205
E-mail: nancystorer@yahoo.com

**Nebraska Thoroughbred
Breeders Association Inc.**
P.O. Box 2215
Grand Island, NE 68802
(308) 384-4683
E-mail: ntbai@kdsi.net

**Thoroughbred Breeders'
Association of New Jersey**
444 N. Ocean Blvd., Second Floor
Ursula Plaza
Long Branch, NJ 07740
(732) 870-9718
E-mail: info@njbreds.com
www.njbreds.com

**New Mexico Horse
Breeders' Association**
P.O. Box 36869
Albuquerque, NM 87176-6869
(505) 262-0224
E-mail: nmhba@worldnet.att.net
www.nmhorsebreeders.com

**New York Thoroughbred
Breeding & Development Fund**
One Penn Plaza, Suite 725
New York, NY 10119
(212) 465-0660
E-mail: nybreds@nybreds.com
www.nybreds.com

**New York Thoroughbred
Horsemen's Association**
P.O. Box 170070,
Jamaica, NY 11417
(718) 848-5045
E-mail: nytha@aol.com
www.nytha.com

**North Carolina
Thoroughbred Breeders
Association**
2103 Orange Factory Road
Bahama, NC 27503
(919) 471-0131

**Ohio Thoroughbred
Breeders & Owners
Association**
6024 Harrison Ave.,
Suite 13
Cincinnati, OH 45248
(513) 574-5888
E-mail: gb.otbo@fuse.net

**Oklahoma Thoroughbred
Association**
2000 S.E. 15th St.,
Bldg. 450, Ste. A
Edmond, OK 73013
(405) 330-1006
E-mail: otawins@aol.com
www.otawins.com

**Oregon Thoroughbred
Breeders Association**
P.O. Box 17248
Portland, OR 97217-0248
E-mail: otba@mindspring.com
www.thoroughbredinfo.com/
showcase/otba.htm

**Pennsylvania Horse
Breeders Association**
701 East Baltimore Pike,
Ste. C-1
Kennett Square, PA 19348
(610) 444-1050
E-mail: execsec@pabred.com
www.pabred.com

**Tennessee Thoroughbred Owners
and Breeders Association**
P.O. Box 158504
Nashville, TN 37215
(615) 254-3376

**Texas Thoroughbred
Association**
P.O. Box 14967, Austin, TX 78761
(512) 458-6133
E-mail:
info@texasthoroughbred.com
www.texasthoroughbred.com

**Virginia Thoroughbred
Association**
38 Garrett St.
Warrenton, VA 20186
(540) 347-4313
E-mail: vta@vabred.org
www.vabred.org

**Washington Thoroughbred
Breeders Association**
P.O. Box 1499
Auburn, WA 98071-1499
E-mail: maindesk@washington-
thoroughbred.com
www.washingtonthoroughbred.com

**West Virginia Thoroughbred
Breeders Association**
P.O. Box 626
Charles Town, WV 25414
(304) 728-6868

Magazines and Supplements

The Blood-Horse magazine
The Blood-Horse *Source*
The Blood-Horse *Auction Edge*
The Blood-Horse *MarketWatch*
The Blood-Horse *Stallion Register*
The Blood-Horse *Auctions*
The Blood-Horse *Nicks*
The Blood-Horse *Sires*
The Blood-Horse *Dams*

Books

Kirkpatrick, Arnold.
*Investing in Thoroughbreds:
Strategies for Success.* Lexington, Ky.:
Eclipse Press, 2001.

Loving, Nancy, DVM.
Conformation and Performance.
Ossining, N.Y.: Breakthrough
Publishers, 1997.

Metzel, Howard.
  Own a Racehorse Without Spending a Fortune. Lexington, Ky.: Eclipse Press, 2003.

Oliver, Robert and Bob Langrish.
  A Photographic Guide to Conformation. North Pomfret, Vt.: Trafalgar Square, 2003.

Proctor, Laura, ed.
  New Thoroughbred Owners Handbook. Lexington, Ky.: TOBA/Eclipse Press, 2003.

Staff of *The Blood-Horse*.
  The Blood-Horse Authoritative Guide to Auctions.
  Lexington, Ky.: Eclipse Press, 2005.

Staff of *The Blood-Horse*.
  The Blood-Horse Authoritative Guide to Breeding Thoroughbreds.
  Lexington, Ky.: Eclipse Press, 2006.

Toby, Milton C. and Karen L. Perch, Ph.D.
  Understanding Equine Business Basics. Lexington, Ky.: Eclipse Press, 2001.

Toby, Milton C. and Karen L. Perch, Ph.D.
  Understanding Equine Law. Lexington, Ky.: Eclipse Press, 1999.

Videos

Insider's Guide To Buying Thoroughbreds at Auction.
  The Blood-Horse, 1999.

Experts Guide To Buying Weanlings.
The Blood-Horse, 2000.

Conformation: How To Buy a Winner.
  The Blood-Horse, 1998.

Online Resources

The Blood-Horse
www.bloodhorse.com

Daily Racing Form
www.drf.com

Bloodstock Research Information System
www.brisnet.com

Thoroughbred Daily News
www.thoroughbreddailynews.com

The Jockey Club Information Systems
www.tjcis.com

The Jockey Club Equine Line
www.equineline.com

Thoroughbred Pedigree Query
www.pedigreequery.com

The Greatest Game
www.thegreatestgame.com

National Thoroughbred Racing Association
www.ntra.com

Thoroughbred Owners and Breeders Association
www.toba.org

Glossary

Agent — Someone authorized to conduct business, such as buying or selling horses, for another.

Angular limb deformity — a lack of conformational correctness as a result of developmental problems in the angles of the joints.

Arbitration — a legal hearing of a dispute between two parties by an impartial third party agreed upon by the adversaries.

Auctioneer — a person conducting a public sale of property that will belong to the highest bidder.

Authorized agent form — a notarized document that empowers one person to act on behalf of another during the sale. The document should be on file in the sales office prior to the start of the sale.

Back at the knee — a conformation flaw in which the leg looks like it has a backward arc, most noticeable at the knee.

Barren — a mare that was bred during a breeding season but did not conceive.

Bid board — the sign that displays the selling horse's hip number and also follows the monetary progression of the bidding.

Bid spotter — an employee of the auction company. Bid spotters are scattered around the sales venue and as each horse is auctioned the bid spotters convey the bids made to the auctioneer.

Bidder — a person who seeks to purchase a horse by indicating acceptance of an amount the auctioneer is asking. A bidder may be bidding against other bidders or against a reserve bid.

Black type — a sales catalog designation for stakes winners and stakes-placed horses. Stakes winners are designated by bold-faced capital letters while stakes-placed horses are bold-faced. Not all stakes races are eligible for black-type designation.

Bloodstock agent — a person who specializes in buying and selling horses, breeding seasons, and stallion shares. A bloodstock agent may be enlisted to represent and advise both buyers and sellers.

Book — a designation of one of a number of catalogs for the same sale. Sales with a large number of horses must divide their catalogs into more than one volume. Each volume is designated as a book; e.g., Book 1 may cover hips 1-700; Book 2, hips 701-1440.

Bottom line — a horse's female family.

Breeze — working a horse at a moderate pace; also refers to the workouts that accompany the sales of two-year-olds in training.

Broodmare — a mare that has

been bred and is used for breeding purposes.

Broodmare prospect — a filly or mare that has not been bred but is capable of being used for breeding purposes.

Broodmare sire — the father of the mare in a pedigree line.

Business plan — a realistic assessment of goals along with objectives and a detailed outline of how these goals will be attained.

Buy-back — a horse offered at public auction that did not make its reserve bid and was, therefore, not sold.

Buyer registration form — a document filed with the sales company before the sale allowing credit verification and requesting approval to buy.

By — used to designate the sire of a particular horse; e.g., Hip #3 is a bay colt *by* Seattle Slew.

Catalog page — the buyer's source of information about each hip number in the sale. A typical catalog page lists the consignor, the hip number, the location of the horse on the sales grounds, the pedigree, sire statistics, maternal bloodlines, etc.

Commission — the fee charged by an agent or sales company for negotiating a transaction. Usually, a commission is a percentage of the sales price.

Conditions of sale — the legal terms that govern how an auction is conducted. These include such things as acceptable methods of payment, warranties and their limitations, resolution of disputes, etc. The conditions of sale will usually be found in the catalog. The conditions of sale also might be announced by the auctioneer prior to each sale session.

Conformation — the way a horse is put together physically.

Consignor — the person or agency responsible for offering a horse for sale at auction.

Corporation — a legal entity created under the authority of a state's laws. The corporation is owned by investor shareholders, who put at risk the amount of their investment but who generally are not personally liable for debts incurred by the business. Corporations can be one of two types, "C" corporations or "S" corporations, whose differences include tax treatment by the Internal Revenue Service.

Credit request — a document submitted to the sales company prior to the sale that authorizes the sales company to check credit.

Dam — a horse's mother.

Drop of the hammer — the act of the auctioneer pounding his gavel and indicating the final bid. The drop of the hammer is usually accompanied by the auctioneer announcing, "Sold."

Female family — the mother's pedigree line from female generation to female generation all the way back to the original ancestress.

Full brother — a male horse that has the same sire and dam as other horses. The famous sires Bull Dog and Sir Gallahad III were full brothers, both being by Teddy out of Plucky Liege.

Full sister — a female horse that has the same sire and dam as other horses.

Gavel — the hammer used by the auctioneer to punctuate the auctioning process.

General partnership — two or more individuals coming together to operate an unincorporated business for a profit.

Graded race — a classification of select races in North America and patterned after the European group races. These races are categorized as grade I, grade II, and grade III. For example, the Kentucky Derby is a grade I event.

Group race — a classification of select races in Europe and other parts of the world such as Australia, etc. These races are categorized as group I, group II, and group III. For example, the Epsom Derby, Prix de l'Arc de Triomphe, and Melbourne Cup are group I events.

Half brother — a male horse that has the same dam as other horses but a different sire. For example, Belmont winner A.P. Indy and Preakness winner Summer Squall are half brothers, both being out of Weekend Surprise, but A.P. Indy is by Seattle Slew and Summer Squall is by Storm Bird.

Half sister — a female horse that has the same dam as other horses but a different sire.

Hip number — how horses are referred to during a sale. The term derives from a sticker with a number on it being placed on each horse's hip as a means of identifying it. The number corresponds to the corresponding lot number in the catalog. For example, Hip #1 will be the first horse in the catalog and the first horse to be sold in the ring.

Holding area — the part of the sales pavilion where the horses are kept before entering the auction ring. This area often gives prospective buyers a last chance to inspect a horse.

Horse of racing age — any Thoroughbred two and older that is eligible to compete in racing.

In foal — a mare is said to be "in foal" when she is pregnant.

Inbred — having one or more common ancestors within the first five generations. In a five-cross pedigree if the name Northern Dancer appears in the third generation on the sire's side of the pedigree and in the fourth generation on the dam's side, the horse is said to be inbred 3 x 4 to Northern Dancer.

Inspection — prior to a sale, prospective buyers have the opportunity to go to the consignor's barn on the sales ground and look over any horses that have piqued their interest. The catalog should specify the times and the dates for inspection.

Limited liability company — a business entity that combines aspects of a partnership (pass-through taxation) and a corporation (limited liability). It is available in some but not all states.

Limited partnership — an unincorporated business owned by two or more individuals, at least one of whom serves as a limited partner. The general partner operates the business and is liable personally for the debts of the business. The limited partner contributes a specific amount of capital to the business, the amount of which establishes the limit of his or her personal liability of business debts. The limited partners do not take an active part in the operation of the business.

Listed race — those stakes races just below graded and group races in quality. These races are designated by [L] on the catalog page.

Mare — a female horse five years old and older or a younger female horse that has been bred.

Out — a horse that has been withdrawn from the sale. The list of outs can be found on the Web site prior to the sale, or a list of the day's outs can be picked up at the sales office. So, before you trek all the way to Barn 48 to inspect Hip #1033 on that cold, windy, wet day, check the list of outs to see if the horse is still in.

Out of — used to designate the dam of a particular horse. For example, Secretariat was a chestnut colt by Bold Ruler *out of* Somethingroyal.

Outcross — having no common ancestors within the first five generations. Of the sixty-two horses in a five-cross pedigree, there will be no duplicated names.

Pavilion — the building where the sale is held.

Partnership agreement — a legal contract that establishes business and sets out the rights and obligations of the partners.

Pedigree — the family tree, listing all the horse's ancestors by generation. Most catalog pages have a three-cross pedigree.

Periosteal transection — a common surgical method used to correct a crooked limb. A small incision is made on the concave side of the limb just above the growth plate, allowing the bone on the slower growing side to catch up to the faster-growing bone on the convex side.

Pinhook — buying a horse in hopes of selling it later at a higher price. For example, many weanlings are purchased to be resold as yearlings.

Precociousness — the early maturity of horses, allowing them to get to the races as two-year-olds.

Produce record — the listing of the offspring of a mare. The catalog pages for breeding stock sales will have a produce record for the mares being sold.

Registration certificate — the document that acts as the "title" to the horse. Originally issued by

The Jockey Club, it passes from owner to owner with the sale of the horse.

Repository — the area on the sales grounds where X-rays and other medical information are kept for inspection.

Reserve — the minimum price set by the seller for a horse at auction.

RNA — the letters used in the results sheet to indicate that a horse did not reach its reserve price (reserve not attained).

Restricted race — a stakes race below the graded, group level that has certain stipulations involved. For example, the stakes may be limited to Florida-bred horses only. These races are designated in the sales catalogs by an [R].

Sales catalog — the guide to the horses being sold. All that's missing is a photo. A page is devoted to each horse entered in the sale and gives pertinent information concerning pedigree, race record, etc. The catalog also includes the conditions of sale. It may also include a guide to local restaurants and hotels.

Scoping — a procedure in which a veterinarian uses an endoscope to examine a horse's upper airway.

Select sale — a sale that is limited to horses chosen on pedigree and conformation.

Sire — a horse's father.

Sire blurb — the part of the catalog page that lists the sire's statistics and achievements.

Sire line — the stallion's pedigree line from generation to generation. For example, Secretariat is by Bold Ruler, who is by Nasrullah, who is by Nearco, etc. Sire lines trace back to one of three original stallions: Eclipse, Herod, or Matchem.

Slipped — used to describe a mare that aborted her foal.

Sole proprietorship — a business owned and operated by a single individual.

Sound — a term used to describe a horse that is free from injury.

Stable release — the document that is necessary to remove a horse from the sales grounds.

Stakes race — a race for which an owner must pay a fee or a series of fees to run. Many stakes are the feature races on a track's racecard. Graded and group races are the highest echelon of stakes races.

Stakes-placed — a term that refers to a horse that finishes second or third in a stakes race.

Stallion — a male horse used for breeding.

Stallion season — the right to mate a mare to a stallion during one breeding year.

Stallion share — a proprietary interest in a stallion, giving the owner the right to breed a mare to a stallion every breeding season for as long as the share is owned or to sell that right to another. Sometimes owning a share in a stallion will result in a bonus season during a breeding year, which allows the owner to breed a second mare to that stallion.

Ticket — the document that acts as a binding contract that the buyer will purchase that hip number at that price, so don't sign the ticket without checking the hip number and the price or else that lovely gray filly you thought you bought for a song may turn out to be a not-so-lovely bay that cost your entire budget.

Toe in — a conformation flaw in which the front of the foot faces inward, giving a pigeon-toed appearance. This flaw often causes the leg to swing outward as the horse travels, a motion known as paddling.

Toe out — a conformation flaw in which the front of the foot faces outward. This flaw often causes the leg to swing inward as the horse travels, a motion known as winging.

Transphyseal bridging — a procedure used to correct angular limb deformities by using screws, staples, or wires to stop growth on one side of the growth plate and allow the other side to catch up.

Two-year-old in training — a sale for juvenile horses that are in the early stages of being readied for racing.

Under-tack show — public breezes of those juveniles entered in two-year-olds in training sales and presented by the sales companies for the benefit of the buyers.

Upright — a conformation flaw in which the pasterns have too little of an angle. The more upright a horse is the more it looks like it is standing on its toes.

Upset price — the minimum price needed to open the bidding on a horse offered at auction.

Warranty — a legal term referring to the representation that the goods will perform as promised. The conditions of sale found in the catalog outline the warranties of the sale and their limitations.

Weanling — a foal that is no longer dependent upon its dam.

X-ray — radiographs on file in the repository. Veterinarians read these radiographs to advise clients on purchases.

Yearling — a horse that has reached its first birthdate. Thoroughbreds become a year older on January 1, the universal birthdate for all Thoroughbreds.

Also in This Series

The Blood-Horse Authoritative Guide to Breeding Thoroughbreds

A complex enterprise such as breeding Thoroughbred racehorses needs a good handbook, especially for the novice owner. *The Blood-Horse Authoritative Guide to Breeding Thoroughbreds* is just such a tool. It lays a solid foundation for venturing into a complicated and risky undertaking.

The Blood-Horse Authoritative Guide to Auctions

A concise guide to the major Thoroughbred auction companies, types of sales, price ranges, and buying and selling protocols. Includes list of sales companies, glossary, and frequently asked questions.

The Blood-Horse Authoritative Guide to Betting Thoroughbreds

This primer teaches the basics of betting, explaining the types of wagers from simple win, place, or show bets to exotic exactas, trifectas, and daily doubles. Novice bettors will discover the factors that many seasoned veterans use to pick their horses — from the condition of the track to work-out times to speed figures.

To order, visit www.ExclusivelyEquine.com or call (800) 582-5604.